CALPURNIA

CALPURNIA

AUDREY DWYER

PLAYWRIGHTS CANADA PRESS
TORONTO

Calpurnia © Copyright 2023 by Audrey Dwyer
First edition: May 2023
Printed and bound in Canada by Imprimerie Gauvin, Gatineau

Cover art by Joy Richu
Cover design by Taryn Dufault / troubleplays.com
Author photo © Cylla Von Tiedemann

Playwrights Canada Press
202-269 Richmond St. w., Toronto, ON M5V 1X1
416.703.0013 | info@playwrightscanada.com | www.playwrightscanada.com

For professional or amateur production rights, please contact:
Colin Rivers, Marquis Entertainment
PO Box 47026, Eaton Centre, Toronto, ON M5B 2P9
416-573-6695 | info@mqent.ca

LIBRARY AND ARCHIVES CANADA CATALOGUING IN PUBLICATION
Title: Calpurnia / Audrey Dwyer.
Names: Dwyer, Audrey, author.
Description: First edition. | A play.
Identifiers: Canadiana (print) 20230184715 | Canadiana (ebook) 2023018474X
 | ISBN 9780369104311 (softcover) | ISBN 9780369104328 (PDF)
 | ISBN 9780369104335 (EPUB)
Classification: LCC PS8607.W92 C35 2023 | DDC C812/.6—dc23

Playwrights Canada Press operates on land which is the ancestral home of the Anishinaabe Nations (Ojibwe / Chippewa, Odawa, Potawatomi, Algonquin, Saulteaux, Nipissing, and Mississauga), the Wendat, and the members of the Haudenosaunee Confederacy (Mohawk, Oneida, Onondaga, Cayuga, Seneca, and Tuscarora), as well as Metis and Inuit peoples. It always was and always will be Indigenous land.

We acknowledge the financial support of the Canada Council for the Arts, the Ontario Arts Council (OAC), Ontario Creates, and the Government of Canada for our publishing activities.

Calpurnia is dedicated to my parents,
Radley and Dahlia Dwyer.

PLAYWRIGHT'S NOTES

The Gordons find comfort in love as they navigate the difficult journey of grief. From the sun's rise, this Mother's Day has a different feel to it.

I thought about the Gordons as a family unit for a long time. A multitude of Black families inspired me. Their doors are always open for others. Long nights of laughter and game playing, sharing rich histories and advice-giving. To be in was a cherished gift. To be chosen was an honour. These families had unique relationships with other marginalized people rooted in understanding and somewhat similar struggles. I remember witnessing abundant generosity and care. I remember what made those families so compassionate and kind to everyone that entered their homes.

Lawrence Gordon is like many older Black men I know. Loving, supportive, and ready to listen. Lawrence's long years of work as a lawyer and then later as a judge enabled him to see so many ways of living. He brings that awareness and more into his home and interactions. Compassion and kindness come from so many places. His lived experience translates into his actions today.

Although the Gordons are high-status, they are not immune from experiencing anti-Black racism and microaggressions. The experience takes one on an emotional journey to say the least. One can be doing their thing. Then the event happens. Sometimes there is shock followed by a full and expansive journey. Sometimes the expansion includes bewilderment, anger, laughter, horror, and tears. Sometimes it includes wonder, curiosity, a physical reaction, and more. There is no order to the expansive part, of course. The feelings come as they come.

I've embedded this journey in the action of the play for audiences to experience by using drama and comedy and a dash of farce. *Calpurnia* runs on the razor's edge of all three. The drama is obvious throughout. There isn't anything hilarious about the experience of racism, prejudice, or ignorance. It is important to recognize the difference between all three. It is also important to recognize the difference and consider power and intersectionality. How does intersectionality reveal itself in the Gordon household? Who feels like a refuge and when? Is one's perception influenced by social context? How does lived experience inform how one acts in high-stress situations? How do the strict rules of social etiquette inform the character's choices?

The comedy is yours to explore. I invite you to discover the awkwardness that these characters endure. I invite you to use group reactions, spit takes, and more. I've embedded the play with physical labour that is relentless and ongoing. I've written a spectacle that grows and builds. I invite you to turn the dial up, amp up, ramp up. Urgency, tension, and obstacles are your friends. The actors need to stay grounded while keeping a high pace. Find that dash of farce and explore.

As Julie discovers her interpretation of a caricature, she sees the world through a new lens. She tries things based on her research, making discoveries along the way. She learns as she goes.

Time is on no one's side. There is an edge in the air this Mother's Day. Breath is held tightly. Anger visits. Tip too far into anger, not funny. Tip too far from anger, it may not feel honest. Keep the tension taut, stay light on your feet (and your heart), and make the physical choices big.

Comedy is hard. Comedy is exhausting. Comedy is rewarding and is an agent of social change. Have fun!

—Audrey Dwyer, May 2023

Calpurnia was first produced by Nightwood Theatre and Sulong Theatre at Buddies in Bad Times Theatre, Toronto, from January 14 to February 4, 2018, with the following cast and creative team:

Julie Gordon: Meghan Swaby
Mark Gordon: Matthew Brown
Lawrence Gordon: Andrew Moodie
Christine Charter: Natasha Greenblatt
James Thompson: Don Allison
Precy Cabigting: Carolyn Fe

Director: Audrey Dwyer
Set Design: Anna Treusch
Costume Design: Jackie Chau
Lighting Design: Bonnie Beecher
Sound Design: Johnny Salib
Props Coordinator: Christine Urquhart
Assistant Set Design: Megan Cinel
Assistant Director: Tsholo Khalema
Stage Manager: Christina Cicko
Assistant Stage Manager: Neha Ross
Production Manager: Suzie Balogh
Assistant Production Manager: Adriana DeAngelis

The play was later remounted in a production by the National Arts Centre English Theatre, the Royal Manitoba Theatre Centre, and Black Theatre Workshop at the John Hirsch Mainstage, Winnipeg, from March 24 to April 16, 2022, and at the Babs Asper Theatre, Ottawa, from April 27 to May 7, 2022, with the following cast and creative team:

Julie Gordon: Emerjade Simms
Mark Gordon: Kwaku Adu-Poku
Lawrence Gordon: Ray Strachan
Christine Charter: Ellie Ellwand
James Thompson: Arne MacPherson
Precy Cabigting: Rochelle Kives

Director: Sarah Garton Stanley
Set Design: Rachel Forbes
Costume Design: Joseph Abetria
Lighting Design: Hugh Conacher
Sound Design: Chris Coyne
Cultural Consultant: Hazel Venzon
Assistant Director: Nikki Shaffeeullah
Assistant Designer: Shauna Jones
Stage Manager: Michael Duggan
Assistant Stage Manager: Zahra Larche

CHARACTERS

Julie Gordon: twenties, Canadian-born, joyful, passionate, sheltered

Lawrence Gordon: fifties to sixties, Jamaican-born, Canadian-raised, kind, authoritarian

Mark Gordon: late twenties, Canadian-born, warm-hearted, private

Precita (Precy) Cabigting: fifties to sixties, born in the Philippines, teasing, direct, fun-loving

Christine Charter: twenties, Canadian-born, anxious, tries hard, quirky, smart, sheltered

James Thompson: late fifties, Canadian-born, life of the party, great dancer, takes up a lot of space

SETTING AND TIME

The Gordon family home, Mother's Day

PUNCTUATION

A forward slash (/) indicates where the next character is to begin speaking their line. This results in an overlap in speech.

An em-dash (—) indicates where the next character begins speaking their line.

NOTES

Keep the pace up. If you choose to not have an intermission, the interlude can take its place. If you choose to have an intermission, you can use all of or parts of the interlude. You can also choose to not do the interlude at all.

TRANSLATION

Ay nako = Oh my God / Wow / Oh no / What / My God / What the MF is going on here?

Ito Na = Here we go

Isang kape o kahit ano lang = I'll have a coffee or something

Hoy = Hey!

Sst = Hey you

Anak = Child

Ano ba = What is going on? (Kind of like the word "eh.")

Ano ba yan = What the heck! / What is that?

Hoy! Bastos yan ha! = Hey! That's perverted!

Pa = too, even, as well

Mag respecto kayo sa akin dito sa itong Bahay nito! Ano ba? = Respect me in this house! What is going on?

Ito nanaman nag mumura ka ulit = Here we are again! You're swearing again!

ACT ONE

We see a large living room in a gorgeous upper-class home. A portrait of Gloria Gordon sits on a wall. Underneath it sits an urn. Beside the urn stands an orchid.

There is a large wooden table. Champagne glasses, cheese knives, napkins, bags of chips, used plates, and leftover food sit on the table. There are bottles of champagne and three shot glasses. One is turned upside down. JULIE *Gordon's laptop is open, playing a song. There is a bar cart that holds expensive Scotches, rum, and liquors; a martini shaker; and glass tumblers. There is a transparent ice bucket on the bar cart with some water in it.*

Two hoodies are littered here and there. There are two armchairs with two side tables beside them. There are glass tumblers, napkins, and food on one of these tables. There is a stack of coasters, but not a single one has been used. Beside the laptop are a few notepads, a manuscript, a bottle of lotion, a lavender essential oil roll-on bottle, a bottle of lavender essential oil spray, and a cup with smoothie remains.

There is a kitchen with modern appliances—a dishwasher and stainless-steel fridge without a magnet in sight. There is an island in the kitchen. There is also a door that leads to the back of the house and a door that leads to the rest of the house.

JULIE *Gordon enters. She is holding five copies of* To Kill a Mockingbird *by Harper Lee. She is wearing an expensive hoodie and sweatpants. Her hood is up over her head. It is 11 a.m. She picks up a wrapped present from the table. She fiddles with it as she watches her laptop screen. She plays a clip from the film* To Kill a Mockingbird, *then opens her copy of* To Kill a Mockingbird. *She reads then . . .*

JULIE: Yes yes yes yes yes yes!

PRECY *Cabigting, the housekeeper, enters from the back door, holding a plastic bag filled with four copies of the Saturday paper.* PRECY *sees a mess in her kitchen.*

PRECY: Ay nako!

JULIE *raises her hands, defensive.* PRECY *enters the living room.*

JULIE: Not me!

PRECY *takes down* JULIE'S *hood.*

PRECY: Good morning, Julie.

JULIE: Good morning, Precy.

PRECY: So windy!

JULIE: Haven't been outside.

PRECY: It's so cold. I don't think summer is coming this year.

She opens the front door and gets the Sunday-morning newspaper.

JULIE: Yeah?

PRECY: It was raining last night.

JULIE: Slept through it.

PRECY: So loud!

JULIE: Yeah?

PRECY: It kept me up all night. And now? Chilly. Chilly. Chilly. Chilly. Chilly.

PRECY watches JULIE work.

Were the lights on all night?

JULIE: . . .

PRECY: I saw the lights on.

JULIE: No, that was me.

PRECY: Early riser.

JULIE: I always wake up early. Not going to church?

PRECY: There's Mark's dinner tonight.

JULIE: No caterers?

PRECY: Why would there be caterers?

JULIE: Sometimes we have caterers?

PRECY: Your dad loves my cooking.

JULIE: We all love your cooking.

PRECY: Your brother loves my cooking.

JULIE: Your cooking is great.

PRECY: You don't like my cooking?

JULIE: Your cooking is my favourite cooking: I love your cooking, your cooking is great!

PRECY: Ahhhhh. Will there be caterers? Will there be caterers? Not for something like this. This is a small dinner.

JULIE: Okay, Precy.

PRECY: Just five people.

JULIE: Okay, Precy.

PRECY: Will there be caterers?

JULIE: I was just / asking.

PRECY: Ay! Will there be caterers . . . I can cook for your brother and an important meal for special people.

JULIE: I hope you get Monday off.

PRECY: Oh! I am *not working* on Monday.

> *PRECY pulls out the newspapers from the plastic bag and puts all four of them on a side table. She puts the Sunday paper underneath the others.*

JULIE: Crappy that you're working on your day off.

PRECY: You're telling me.

JULIE: Can't go to church.

PRECY: I know.

JULIE: Mother's Day.

PRECY: I know!

JULIE: Another reason why I think this dinner shouldn't be happening.

PRECY: Hahaha! You don't want to go, ha?

JULIE: Mmm . . . I'm just in a great place in my research! It's going well!

> *Silence as* JULIE *continues working.* PRECY *takes off her jacket and scarf. She hangs both in the closet by the front door. She puts her purse in there too. She holds the empty plastic bag. She sees the present on the table.*

PRECY: Hoy! A present!

> *She picks it up.*

Oh! For you! From Christine. Ooooooooo! Nice ribbon!

JULIE: . . .

PRECY: Not your birthday!

JULIE: . . .

PRECY: *(teasing)* Feels like a book of handwritten love poems.

JULIE: . . .

It's a copy of *To Kill a Mockingbird*. It's a thing we do.

PRECY: Ohhhh . . .

(re: the mess in the house) O! Big party here!

JULIE: Mark and Christine slept over last night.

PRECY: OoOooh.

JULIE: Yep.

PRECY: Celebration!

JULIE: Yep.

PRECY: *(dancing)* Party party!

JULIE: Yep.

PRECY: Did you party party?

> *JULIE gives PRECY a look.*

JULIE: I was sound asleep.

> *Silence as JULIE returns to her work. PRECY clears off the table—two wooden cutting boards with cheese remains and dry bread edges. PRECY takes the cutting boards to the kitchen. She puts the plastic bag in a drawer. Then—*

PRECY: When was the last time I saw your brother?

JULIE: I don't know, Precy. When was the last time you saw my brother?

PRECY: Christine and Mark got a place! You see it?

JULIE: Nope!

PRECY: Oh, sorry I—

JULIE: Deadline!

PRECY: Okay, okay, okay. Sorry. Sorry.

    Silence. PRECY *begins working again then—*

(*alarmed*) O!

JULIE: Are you / okay?!

PRECY: O!!

JULIE: Is / everything—

PRECY: Ay! The / lumpia!!!

JULIE: The—

PRECY: Lumpia!! Your dad wanted lumpia! I was going to make some! I forgot!

JULIE: Oh my God, Precy / I thought you—

PRECY: I completely forgot!

JULIE: You don't have time to make lumpia?

PRECY: Ay, not today. I'll have to buy some.

JULIE: Buy some?

PRECY: I have no time!

    JULIE gives her a look.

You can't tell the difference.

JULIE: I can.

PRECY: No.

JULIE: Yes I can.

PRECY: No.

JULIE: Uh. *Yes.*

PRECY: I'm a good cook?

JULIE: Yes.

PRECY: Better than Carmela's Kitchen?

Meghan Swaby as Julie and Carolyn Fe as Precy. Produced by Nightwood Theatre and Sulong Theatre. Set Design: Anna Treusch, Costume Design: Jackie Chau, Lighting Design: Bonnie Beecher. Photo by Dahlia Katz.

JULIE: Yeah.

PRECY: You mean it?

JULIE: Yeah.

PRECY: You promise?

JULIE: You are way better than Carmela's Kitchen.

PRECY: Ay! Okay. I won't buy them from Carmela!

JULIE returns to her work.

Sorry, Carmela, mine are better than yours!!

Beat.

Next time, write a movie about *Filipina* maids! Starring . . .

She holds a dramatic pose.

JULIE: . . .

She drops the pose.

PRECY: You have to eat!

(disgusted) Smoothie.

PRECY takes the cup.

JULIE: Isang kape o kahit ano lang.

PRECY: *(disgusted)* Isang kape o kahit ano lang?

(*under her breath*) Ano ba yan! Eat! Not just coffee. So, you want some eggs?

(*teasing*) Glad to see you working though. Not just sleeping.

JULIE: Just because I'm in my room doesn't mean I'm sleeping.

PRECY: (*teasing*) Oh, no? Really? You and your computer.

> PRECY *picks up* To Kill a Mockingbird *and flips through it. She stops at the first page.*

So many secrets about your movie.

(*reading*) Ooo. That's so sweet. Oh ohhh. This is a very sweet message. Very sweet.

> JULIE *takes the book from* PRECY.

JULIE: Christine wants to help me research, so she buys me a book for each character. And she writes nice things on the inside.

PRECY: So?

JULIE: She keeps buying me copies and she wants me to credit her when we shoot the film.

PRECY: That's nice!

> *Beat.*

Are you going to give me a credit? You ask me all those questions all the time—I deserve a credit.

JULIE: You'll be in the thank yous. You know what? Read it.

JULIE hands her one of the copies on the table.

PRECY: This? I don't have time for this.

JULIE: Pretty please! I'll interview you after you read it.

PRECY: Ha! You're joking!

JULIE: It'll take an hour, tops.

PRECY: An "hour"? "Tops"? You think I have an "hour" "tops"?

JULIE: (*sweetly*) I think you do.

PRECY: You think I have time for an interview *and* to read this book?

JULIE: Read it in your downtime?

PRECY: Downtime?!

JULIE: Before you go to bed or something.

PRECY: Anak, the last time I read before bed was when I would read to you and then tuck you in!

JULIE: Please nooo . . .

PRECY: (*teasing*) Oh you with your little braids and your rosy cheeks and your little teeth. So smart! Blue duck, yellow duck, quack, quack, quack.

JULIE: I was five.

PRECY: (*firm*) Hoy! You were four!

JULIE: So? Read it in your downtime.

PRECY: You think I have downtime? You think I have downtime?

PRECY goes to the closet and puts the book in her purse.

You read everything. My magazines, the Bible, Christmas cards. I could not believe it.

JULIE: Are you going to let me write down here or what?

PRECY: (*teasing*) What's the matter? I can't talk to you? Why don't you work upstairs? Ohhh! Okay.

JULIE: What?

PRECY: You know. Caressing. Lovemaaaaking.

JULIE: Oh my God!

PRECY: Sst! It's the Lord's day!

JULIE: Don't make me think about— Oh my God!!

PRECY: I have to work on a Sunday and hear this language?

JULIE: Okay, ugh, sorry!

JULIE starts packing up her laptop and supplies to work upstairs.

PRECY: Not on my watch! On my day off? No thank you!

Beat.

Are you still going on a trip with Christine? Stay out of the sun! Oo! Bad mood. Okay okay.

PRECY exits into the kitchen with the ice bucket and starts to clean. CHRISTINE enters wearing pyjamas. She has a scrapbook. PRECY turns on the kettle for CHRISTINE. She gets a lemon from a bowl filled with lemons, cuts it, and puts a slice in a mug. She adds fresh mint from a glass filled with sprigs of mint.

CHRISTINE: Hey! I knocked on your door! We missed you last night!

CHRISTINE hugs JULIE.

You should have come down.

PRECY: Good morning, Christine!

CHRISTINE: Morning! Oooo, this is different.

JULIE: Yes.

CHRISTINE: I like it!

They do the physical game they always do when CHRISTINE tries and knows not to touch JULIE's hair. An old routine between them.

So, are you just like writing all the time?

JULIE: Pretty much.

CHRISTINE: How's it all going?

JULIE: I'm in a great place, just got this deadline . . .

CHRISTINE: I have a question about your movie.

JULIE: Is it a racial question?

CHRISTINE: Why do you think it would be a racial question?

JULIE: Because it usually is a racial question?

CHRISTINE: So it is a racial question?

JULIE: So maybe later?

> JULIE *makes her way upstairs.* CHRISTINE *picks up her gift.*

CHRISTINE: Lee Lee!

PRECY: Hot water with a lemon slice and fresh mint!

CHRISTINE: Thank you. Open. Opennnn it!

> JULIE *returns to the table.*

JULIE: Thanks, you.

CHRISTINE: Read what I wrote. Come on, read it!

JULIE: Later, later.

CHRISTINE: Come onnnn. After biking, maybe? Do you wanna come biking? Come biking with us! Come on! You never come out!

> JULIE *heads upstairs again.* LAWRENCE *Gordon,* JULIE'*s dad, enters, talking on his phone. He speaks in a Jamaican accent. It is a bad one because he rarely, if ever, uses one. As* LAWRENCE *enters, he brings* JULIE *back into the living room and kisses her on the forehead.*

LAWRENCE: Mm hmmm . . . Mmmm hmmm . . . Yes, I understand that . . . Yes, I understand that as well . . . Absolutely . . .

JULIE and CHRISTINE note that his accent is bad. LAWRENCE flips through the newspaper. CHRISTINE hands him the section with the article about MARK.

Yes, Mother's Day. Yes, I *absolutely understand* that taking a husband and father away from his wife and daughters on Mother's Day means that I'm going to have to have you all over for some Jamaican food sometime during the summer, and yes, I *absolutely understand* that that means jerk chicken, rum punch, and—pardon me? I'm sorry?

He hands JULIE the section of the paper. They are playful. He rubs his head in pain.

Of course there will be Beres Hammond, *of course there will be.* Thank you, Tonya. Tell Thompson I'll see him later tonight. All right. Thank you. Thank you. Yes. Thank you. Talk to you soon, Tonya. Of course, *happy Mother's Day.* Take care. Goodbye.

A beat. He drops the accent.

Jamaicans!

You doing all right, Christine?

CHRISTINE: Uh huh.

PRECY heads to the laundry room. CHRISTINE sits and reads the paper.

LAWRENCE: *(to JULIE)* Dinner. Seven.

JULIE: Not going.

LAWRENCE: My little love bug.

JULIE: Gotta work.

LAWRENCE: I want you to know this for tonight.

JULIE: Can't, Dad.

LAWRENCE: Thompson just confirmed.

JULIE: He *just* confirmed?

LAWRENCE: He's a busy guy.

JULIE: You're a busy guy. Does Mark know you're a busy guy?

LAWRENCE: *(under his breath)* Sh!

    LAWRENCE checks if MARK is going to enter the room.

JULIE: Unbelievable! You tell *me* when you hook *me* up.

    CHRISTINE looks up from her paper.

LAWRENCE: You have less . . . pride.

JULIE: Wow.

LAWRENCE: Your brother's a man.

JULIE: Wow.

LAWRENCE: Your brother's a man.

JULIE: Please please don't call him a man.

LAWRENCE: And / men—

JULIE: Men—

JULIE & LAWRENCE: Men don't like to know they're being helped.

LAWRENCE: Don't— He has done so much for you.

As JULIE *mimics* LAWRENCE, LAWRENCE *speeds up.*

He taught you how to / ride your bike, how to look both ways—

JULIE: Ride your bike, how to look both ways—

JULIE & LAWRENCE: Science, math. Grade three. He helped you come in third place during the science fair. The volcano? All him. And what about . . . what about . . .

JULIE *gives him a look.*

LAWRENCE: The spelling bee.

JULIE: Oh for real? You're going—

LAWRENCE: He coached you for weeks. Medical textbooks, Oxford English dictionaries, the one with the magnifying glass. He even came up with a pre-competition ritual to calm your nerves, and he introduced you to lavender essential oil.

JULIE: It worked—it really did.

JULIE *gets her lavender lotion, opens it, and smells it. She lotions up her arms and hands.*

LAWRENCE: *Lavandula angustifolia.*

JULIE: How do you know—

LAWRENCE: Spell it.

JULIE: *Lavandula . . .*

LAWRENCE: *Lavandula angustifolia.*

JULIE stands.

JULIE: *Lavandula angustifolia.*

(*quickly*) L-A-V-A-N-D-U-L-A A-N-G-U-S-T-I-F-O-L-I-A.

CHRISTINE: Woo!

LAWRENCE: See what I'm saying?

JULIE: These aren't hard words for me to—

During his speech, JULIE tosses CHRISTINE the lotion. She smells it and the puts some on her hands, arms, and neck.

LAWRENCE: *Lavandula angustifolia.* You love words. Mark nurtured that. The only thing I'm asking you to do is attend a very short dinner, in your own home, eat a delicious meal with us, fix yourself up. Who knows, maybe you might learn something about what you're writing? And Thompson will get to see us as a family.

JULIE: And then you're going to get Thompson to insert Mark into his firm.

LAWRENCE: Sh!

LAWRENCE taps JULIE with the newspaper.

He can do better in a better firm.

JULIE: The article.

LAWRENCE: Yes?

JULIE: Yes?!

LAWRENCE: Yes.

JULIE: Yes.

LAWRENCE: Yes, Julie, the answer is yes.

JULIE: Wowwwww.

LAWRENCE: It's nothing major and Mark's feeling happy about it.

CHRISTINE: Did something happen because of the article?

JULIE: So why do we even need this dinner?

LAWRENCE: A meeting over dinner. It's civil.

JULIE: You hooked him up with the job. It's not like this Thompson guy is gonna say no.

LAWRENCE: *(re: her volume)* Can you—

JULIE: Control freak.

LAWRENCE: Excuse me?

JULIE: Just get Thompson to call him and tell him he starts on Monday.

LAWRENCE: The men will talk, have a drink, have some food. I can't just tell people what to do. Except for you.

(*to* CHRISTINE) And also you.

JULIE *picks up the paper with two fingers.*

CHRISTINE: You paid someone to write this?

LAWRENCE: Had Mark interviewed, yes.

CHRISTINE: Whoa.

JULIE: I know. Mark isn't *that* good.

CHRISTINE: . . .

LAWRENCE: We all need to know it for tonight. We will be talking about it tonight.

JULIE: You all will be talking about it tonight. I will be writing in my bedroom upstairs.

LAWRENCE: If Mark's around the best, he'll become the best. First firm. His choice. Starter firm. Fine . . . suitable.

CHRISTINE: He loved his first firm.

LAWRENCE: Second firm. My choice.

JULIE: (*to* CHRISTINE) How did he get into these firms, you ask?

CHRISTINE: We prepped for both interviews.

JULIE: That's really sweet.

CHRISTINE: We prepped for this dinner. He's so nervous.

LAWRENCE: He knows . . .

CHRISTINE: Yeah, I mean, he knows being your son . . . but he doesn't know know. We rehearse the interview process. We lose sleep. We didn't sleep last night! "Thirty under thirty . . . "

JULIE: You choose that photo?

CHRISTINE: He's very proud—

JULIE: . . .

CHRISTINE: We've been working on this!

JULIE picks up the scrapbook and laughs.

JULIE: What twenty-eight-year-old grown man scrapbooks?

CHRISTINE: Vision-boarding.

JULIE: But it's in a—

LAWRENCE: Today is your opportunity . . .

JULIE is still laughing.

JULIE: One sec, one sec— "To build the tomorrow you want."

LAWRENCE: Thank you.

JULIE: Except that you build the tomorrow that Mark doesn't want.

LAWRENCE: He wants this.

JULIE laughs. CHRISTINE takes the scrapbook.

CHRISTINE: Ohhhhh, he really wants this!

JULIE: Does he want to know that *you* want this so much—so so so so so much—that *you* put it all together for him *all the time*?

LAWRENCE: Sh! Some kids need a little push.

JULIE: A *little* push?

> *PRECY re-enters. She sees CHRISTINE and offers her a pillow, which she doesn't take.*

PRECY: Good morning, Mr. Gordon. How are you today?

LAWRENCE: Hungover. Can you get me some Aspirin please?

PRECY: Yes, Mr. Gordon.

LAWRENCE: Two.

PRECY: Yes, Mr. Gordon.

> *PRECY leaves to get Aspirin.*

CHRISTINE: *(whispers to herself)* Ohhhh . . . no no no no—I don't want to know this, / I don't want to know this, I don't want to know this!

LAWRENCE: I don't recall any complaints when I *hooked you up* with a Hollywood literary agent.

CHRISTINE: *(whispers to herself)* Why meeee?

JULIE: Whatever, Dad. Completely different scenario, but whatever.

LAWRENCE: No one is telling him about the article.

> *CHRISTINE takes the article.*

CHRISTINE: / (*whispers to herself*) Oh my God, oh my God!

JULIE: I'm not going to tell him. This is all you, Dad.

LAWRENCE: Precious.

JULIE: All. Youuuuuu.

CHRISTINE: Oh my God, no no no no, you guys . . .

LAWRENCE: When you have kids, / you'll understand.

JULIE: Kids?!   **LAWRENCE:** (*to* CHRISTINE) It'll be fine.

LAWRENCE: (*to both*) You'll want everything to be just so.

CHRISTINE: (*whispers*) How am I supposed to hide this from Mark?

JULIE: Welcome to the club.

LAWRENCE: I'm getting old.

JULIE: Nope, no, Dad. You're perfectly healthy.

CHRISTINE: (*more anxious*) ARE YOU OKAY?

JULIE: He's very healthy.

LAWRENCE: Aren't we all dying?

JULIE: Come on.   **CHRISTINE:** NO! You're so strong!

CHRISTINE impulsively touches him, then quickly pulls back. He lightly hits her with the article.

LAWRENCE: I'm healthy! Healthy! / Thank you very much!

CHRISTINE: Sorry!

JULIE: Just a control freak!

> PRECY *returns with a tray—Aspirin on a plate and a glass of water.*

LAWRENCE: Thank you, Precy. And how's your writing going?

JULIE: . . .

LAWRENCE: How much have you written since yesterday?

JULIE: I'm doing research.

LAWRENCE: Research?

JULIE: Yeah, research. Writers research.

LAWRENCE: Procrastinating?

JULIE: No.

LAWRENCE: You sure?

JULIE: *Yes.*

> LAWRENCE *looks at her phone.*

LAWRENCE: You're on TikTok.

JULIE: So?

LAWRENCE: TikTok?

JULIE: There's a lot of information on TikTok.

LAWRENCE: Right.

JULIE: Tons of people are talking about what I'm writing about.

LAWRENCE: Black maids in the 1930s?

JULIE: Anti-racist policies. Race relations in the United States. Protests.

LAWRENCE takes JULIE's phone.

LAWRENCE: Looks like dancing to me.

He adjusts the volume on her phone. Music. He takes a moment and then does the bust down. JULIE, CHRISTINE, and PRECY watch. MARK enters, seeing LAWRENCE's moves. He is wearing pyjamas that match CHRISTINE's.

MARK: We're doing the bust down?

He joins in.

CHRISTINE: Baby!!

LAWRENCE: If you know, you know.

JULIE takes the phone. She turns off the music.

JULIE: (*re: their matching pyjamas*) And choices were made.

She gets back to work.

PRECY: Oooh! Mark!

CHRISTINE hugs MARK and clings on to him. She's a little extra.

Such good news!

MARK: Thanks, Precy.

PRECY: I read the article! Thirty under thirty!

MARK: Yeah, yeah.

PRECY: You're only twenty-eight.

MARK: I know.

PRECY: There are always articles about Black men getting arrested. Not you!

MARK looks at LAWRENCE.

MARK: *(laughing)* Isn't that something?

PRECY: And Saturday? Everybody reads on Saturday. Congratulations!

MARK: Thanks, Precy. Thanks a lot.

(to CHRISTINE) You okay?

PRECY: You want some lunch?

LAWRENCE: Thanks, Precy. We're going biking shortly.

PRECY: Ahhh.

MARK: Water.

LAWRENCE: Water.

JULIE: Coffee.

PRECY exits, taking two champagne bottles. She puts them in recycling. She pours a glass of water for MARK. She prepares a cold compress for LAWRENCE and places it on a tray.

CHRISTINE gives MARK a big hug.

MARK: You should have partied with us last night.

JULIE: Oh yeah?

MARK: Dad brought out the good Scotch.

JULIE: Obviously.

LAWRENCE: A little headache.

MARK: It was the champagne.

CHRISTINE holds MARK's hand.

CHRISTINE: Baby!

PRECY enters with the cold compress for LAWRENCE. He takes the compress. She clears the Aspirin and brings the lotion back to JULIE. She takes three tumblers and the napkin from the side table and exits into the kitchen.

LAWRENCE: I'm fine.

MARK: He's fine.

JULIE: Obviously.

MARK: What's your problem?

JULIE: I don't have a problem.

MARK: (*in patois*) Yu no have no problem?

JULIE: Yep.

MARK: We kept you up.

JULIE: No, I had a great sleep.

MARK: You should have partied with us! We did shots.

JULIE: Obviously.

LAWRENCE: I did two shots.

MARK: Four shots, but who's counting.

>   *JULIE* does a mock stretch.

JULIE: Hi, everyone. Good morning. Hello. You may not have noticed, but I was down here first.

MARK: Did you read my article?

JULIE: And so, since I was down here first, the least you could do is—

MARK: Did you read my article?

JULIE: I would like to write down here, please.

MARK: Did you read my article?

JULIE: Remember when you said—

MARK: I couldn't read your piece—

JULIE: You said you would.

MARK: It was about Mom.

JULIE: For months.

MARK: Yes, but—

JULIE: You're like dandruff. Flaky, white, and everywhere.

MARK picks up the article.

MARK: Good one. New one. Good one. You read this?

JULIE: Of course I did.

MARK: Seriously?

JULIE: Nope.

CHRISTINE takes some space.

MARK: You're coming to the dinner, right?

JULIE: I did read this, though. Thompson will choose you. Your "vision board."

MARK: Scrapbook.

JULIE: Will make. It happen.

MARK: You're coming, right?

JULIE: For sure. I saw the cut-out of me on page two, so yes, I'll be there.

CHRISTINE opens the scrapbook and flips to page two.

Kidding!

JULIE returns to her laptop.

MARK: (*to LAWRENCE*) She's coming.

JULIE: I'm probably not coming, so you all just need to know that.

MARK: You have to read the article, and you're coming to the dinner.

LAWRENCE: Julie.

MARK: We're a team.

JULIE: No we're not.

MARK: (*looks at her computer screen*) You're on Instagram.

JULIE: I'm writing. I have a deadline. I'm busy.

LAWRENCE: She'll be there.

PRECY enters with drinks for MARK and LAWRENCE.

PRECY: (*firm*) Are you sure you're okay for lunch?

LAWRENCE: We're going to have lunch at the park.

PRECY: Okay.

CHRISTINE: Not even a *little bit of biking*?

MARK: Dad.

CHRISTINE: Lee Lee. You're all by yourself all the time.

MARK: We need to be a whole family for this one.

JULIE: Are we getting Team Mark jerseys? Or Team Dad jerseys?

CHRISTINE: I know you're not being serious, but I don't think that's a bad idea.

MARK: You know what I mean.

JULIE: Mother's Day. Team Mark on Mother's Day.

    Beat.

Well. Thank you for all the invitations to all the things. I was given a week to hand over a completely perfected draft and I just want to write it. I *just* want to write it

CHRISTINE: (*alarmed*) Are you coming to St. Barts? I changed the date.

JULIE: For Mark's thing.

CHRISTINE: I paid for the tickets. I can change them again, that's fine, but we're going to St. Barts. We always go to St. Barts.

JULIE: Maybe? I have a deadline—I need to finish this. I have, like, three days left.

CHRISTINE: I can't believe we're not going to St. Barts. We're not going to St. Barts?

(*worried*) Mark?

JULIE saves her document and then closes her laptop. She packs up her things to leave. MARK and CHRISTINE have a moment together. CHRISTINE pulls away from MARK and sits away from him. She returns to reading the article about him. LAWRENCE stands. PRECY goes back into the kitchen and cleans the countertops.

LAWRENCE: How's your treatment?

JULIE: My treatment is perfect.

LAWRENCE: The script?

JULIE: Perfect.

LAWRENCE: You get any notes on your script?

JULIE: Yes.

LAWRENCE: Oh, he read it? I told him he had to read it.

JULIE: I have nothing but gratitude for you, thank you so much.

LAWRENCE: All right, you little brat. He said he had no time. So what did he say about it?

JULIE: Hates it.

LAWRENCE: No! What did he say?

JULIE: Calpurnia isn't active enough. Apparently a *common problem of female writers.* And she sounds too upper-class. Too Canadian. Apparently, too much like me. So, I'm doing research, watching *To Kill a Mockingbird* again. *Working.*

LAWRENCE: Research.

JULIE: I just need. Some time. To focus.

LAWRENCE: Are you bookmarking everything you come across? Because you should be bookmarking everything you come across. Your laptop needs to be archiving every page you touch.

JULIE: Yeah, history does that.

LAWRENCE: You need to be creating an archive of all your research material.

LAWRENCE sits and takes over her laptop. MARK watches.

Are these your drafts?

Beat.

Do you have a folder where you put all your drafts?

JULIE: I know how to make—

LAWRENCE: Here . . . we . . . go . . .

JULIE rubs her temples and neck with the lavender essential oil roll-on bottle.

And then you name it. Calpurnia?

(typing) Caaaalpuuuurnia. There you go.

JULIE: Thank you.

LAWRENCE: Hard name to say. Drafts. In there.

JULIE: Thanks.

LAWRENCE stands. MARK mimics LAWRENCE's expansive gestures behind his back for JULIE's and CHRISTINE's benefit.

LAWRENCE: And when you're brainstorming, do it on a big piece of paper. Write things down on a big piece of paper, because you need to see what you'll be discussing in your work. Write the themes down, the conversations down. How it will go. Use different coloured markers. A starburst approach.

LAWRENCE catches MARK.

Write words. Lines. Other words. Get up on your feet and write it. You're slumping like a . . . I'm signing you up for yoga.

LAWRENCE sits at her laptop, types. JULIE spritzes the air around her with the essential oil spray.

JULIE: I'm not really into yoga.

CHRISTINE looks up from her reading.

CHRISTINE: You love yoga.

JULIE: When I'm in those studios, I just wonder about who's there and who's not.

CHRISTINE: We're doing yoga in St. Barts.

JULIE: Ever wonder about who's there and who's not?

CHRISTINE: Hatha yoga, private sessions, it's booked. You love this. It's already booked.

JULIE: I'm just not into—

LAWRENCE: You need to get organized. You look back at those notes, you know where you started. How you started. When you do interviews, you're going to need to know what inspired you.

LAWRENCE pokes JULIE. JULIE pokes him back, playfully.

JULIE: Thanks.

JULIE gets back into her seat and returns to her work.

LAWRENCE: People are going to ask you what inspired you.

MARK: You should make a movie about Dad.

LAWRENCE: Haha . . . I'm not into all that.

MARK: About his time in law school, how he became a judge.

LAWRENCE: No no no no, I wouldn't be—

MARK: Your big speech . . . Think about it. Denzel Washington. Idris Elba.

CHRISTINE: Idris Elba. Yes!

LAWRENCE: Who would be my co-star?

MARK: Me.

PRECY laughs.

CHRISTINE: Hot!

MARK laughs.

CHRISTINE: (*whispers*) What? No, you'd be brilliant, baby. You're the—

LAWRENCE: (*to* MARK) And as for you, young man. Today is your opportunity . . .

MARK: To build the tomorrow you want. How can I help you, Dad?

LAWRENCE: When *the* James Thompson arrives tonight—

MARK: Nope. Back off.

LAWRENCE: I'll give you an intro . . . talk about who's involved.

MARK: No. No thank you, Dad.

LAWRENCE: Then you'll show him the article, then we'll talk about the case.

MARK: You're not running this. I am running this.

LAWRENCE: You're nervous.

MARK: Not nervous.

LAWRENCE: His team is driven.

MARK: I'm driven.

LAWRENCE: More driven.

MARK: I'm driven.

LAWRENCE: Annoyed?

MARK: Yes, I'm feeling annoyed.

LAWRENCE: This is a big one. One of the most prestigious firms across the country.

MARK: Thanks. Thanks for inviting him over, but *I am running this.*

JULIE: Sounds like you want some independence.

MARK: Sounds like I do.

LAWRENCE's cellphone rings.

LAWRENCE: Heyyyy, Thompson!

LAWRENCE leaves out the front door.

MARK: He's cancelling.

JULIE: Well, it is Mother's Day.

CHRISTINE: He's not cancelling. He's probably just . . . Don't worry about it.

(to JULIE) Every May we go to St. Barts to remember our moms. You're not going to—

MARK: Sorry.

(to JULIE) Mom would be happy that we're spending today *securing* something big for me. *And* she would *appreciate* a feature film about her and Dad. Grandma and Grandpa arrive from Jamaica, Dad as a kid, the racism he faced, teen years, *when he met Mom*, us, their love story, Mom passes, his rise to fame as a lawyer, when he became a judge, his retirement . . .

CHRISTINE: I'd watch that movie. Buuuuuut . . . I'd also watch the movie you're making, Lee Lee!

JULIE: Dad's story is so . . . timid.

CHRISTINE: I read *To Kill a Mockingbird* again. Pretty horrendous.

MARK: It's my favourite book.

CHRISTINE: Really.

MARK: And I love the movie.

CHRISTINE: Really?

MARK: It's my favourite movie.

CHRISTINE: You've never mentioned that before.

MARK: It's a beautiful movie.

CHRISTINE: Why haven't we watched it together?

MARK: I don't know. It's kind of personal.

JULIE: You're not going to like my screenplay.

MARK: I probably won't.

MARK picks up JULIE's treatment.

I'll start with the treatment, if I may.

MARK reads. As CHRISTINE looks at what JULIE is writing—

CHRISTINE: I think the book is better than the movie, but I still don't like the book.

JULIE closes her laptop.

I liked it more when we read it in high school, but I'm not that into it right now.

As JULIE walks into the kitchen to make coffee—

MARK: A scene about how Calpurnia learns to read?

JULIE: Yep.

MARK: Her preacher teaches her how to read?

JULIE: Yep.

MARK: That didn't happen in the book.

JULIE: Ding ding!

JULIE turns on the espresso machine.

MARK: *(reading)* "Calpurnia is at home with her husband and kids."

JULIE: Yep.

CHRISTINE: So intense.

MARK: I'm a lawyer.

CHRISTINE: It's like you're in court.

JULIE: *(playfully)* No interruptions, you.

MARK: Calpurnia. Home. Husband. Kids.

JULIE: I said yep.

MARK: (*reading*) "Flashback to Calpurnia falling in love, getting married . . . "

JULIE: I'm trying to make her more human, less caricature.

MARK: Her mother dies . . . You can't just throw in that her mother dies!

JULIE: Yeah I can.

MARK: That happened to us!

JULIE: So?

MARK: None of those things happened in the book!

> *Silence.* PRECY *enters the living room with a caddy of cleaning supplies. She checks on* CHRISTINE'*s cup. It's good. She cleans, arranges pillows, dusts shelves, and waters the orchid. She wipes down the table.*

Atticus refuses to pay her?

JULIE: Yep.

MARK: That didn't happen.

JULIE: Yeah it did. Some of them didn't get paid.

MARK: Yes, but Atticus was one of the good guys.

JULIE: According to Harper Lee.

MARK: According to Harper Lee.

JULIE: What does she know about being racialized?

MARK: Well, nothing. But she lived during that era—Calpurnia was her maid.

JULIE: Harper Lee isn't a Black housekeeper. How would she know what it was like to be a Black housekeeper?

Slight pause as MARK *scans the document, then—*

MARK: *(reading)* "To save money, she walks to and from work. She walks for miles." Whoa whoa whoa! Calpurnia arrives late and Atticus hits her?

CHRISTINE: Eeee . . . I don't remember that being in the book.

MARK: A little extreme, don't you think?

JULIE: No. Those women weren't treated very well.

MARK: *(reading)* She hides her bruises? This is like torture porn / or something . . .

PRECY: Hoy! / Bastos yan ha!

JULIE: I'm writing about what actually happened to these women. Everybody thinks that these women were happy all the time, that they were members of the family.

Silence as MARK *reads. Then—*

What.

MARK *continues reading.*

Harper Lee. She builds in this intimacy that . . . *from what my research provides* . . . Calpurnia is this "mother figure," right?

MARK: Mammy culture. Yes.

JULIE: Yes, mammy culture! But I'm talking women not getting paid, women being assaulted. Scout and Calpurnia have this mother slash daughter slash friendship, but they didn't know each other!

CHRISTINE: I didn't know my maid. I was nice to her, but I didn't *know know* her.

MARK: Don't force the book to be something it's not.

CHRISTINE: I'm not sure my maid wanted to be my mom or my friend. We're friends now, I think. She's like a mom. Aunt. Maunt.

    CHRISTINE *laughs at her own joke then sharply stops off a look from* JULIE *and* MARK.

JULIE: Calpurnia's a stereotype. That's basically the only thing we learned about her in high school.

CHRISTINE & MARK: Bad Boy Bartko.

MARK: He was tough.

CHRISTINE: You were pretty quiet in English.

MARK: Julie wasn't quiet in high school!

CHRISTINE: She was during English.

JULIE: I wonder why.

CHRISTINE: Remember when he said the N / word—

MARK & JULIE: Don't—

MARK brings CHRISTINE aside.

MARK: Remember what I said about you feeling like you need to help?

CHRISTINE: Too much?

MARK nods.

JULIE: Overwhelming. Rerouting the entire conversation.

CHRISTINE: Okay, but—

JULIE: Intention versus impact.

MARK: *(to CHRISTINE, whispers)* Muffin?

(to Julie) Nope. Round two. Court scene.

JULIE: Court scene. Atticus slut-shames Mayella.

MARK: How?! When?!

JULIE: Mayella is up on trial, he makes her feel *so guilty* for wanting to sleep with a Black man. So what if she wanted to sleep with a Black man? Lots of women want to sleep with Black men.

> *CHRISTINE sits. PRECY offers her the pillow, which she takes. PRECY goes into the kitchen, puts away the cleaning caddy, and prepares some cookies on a plate.*

That's victim blaming.

MARK: Victim blaming? He's just doing his job.

JULIE: Whether Mayella is lying or not, that's Atticus's approach.

MARK: In the book and the film he was smart, clear-headed, determined. "In the name of God!"

JULIE: Do you even believe in God? It's Sunday. It is literally church o'clock right now. If I was a teenager, reading this book, today? If I was a teenager. Reading this book. To. Day. And I wanted to take someone to court? I wouldn't.

MARK: Things have changed for women.

JULIE & CHRISTINE: What?

MARK: You know they have. You *know* they have.

(*to JULIE*) Atticus Finch is an icon!

JULIE: Okay. Atticus Finch, "the icon," wasn't a civil-rights activist.

MARK: He was a lawyer . . .

JULIE: He was doing his job. That's it. He was assigned the case. He *had* to take it.

MARK: He was the top lawyer in the county!

JULIE: Yes, but people think he was a civil-rights activist. An ally.

MARK: So, no allies?

JULIE: (*helpless*) Do we need them? I don't know anymore. / I really don't.

MARK: No allies?

JULIE: (*helpless*) I do so much explaining, online—they don't get it. I'm honestly unsure. Maybe yeah, no allies. Do it ourselves?

MARK: Atticus Finch.

JULIE: He was just doing his job.

MARK: Okay, Twitter academic. Interpretation. We're allowed to interpret and to find meaning. Atticus cared. About his community, his children, and Calpurnia.

He picks up one of the copies of the novel.

He visited Mrs. Robinson. She welcomed him into her home. Unheard of. The whole community witnessed this.

PRECY enters the living room with a plate of cookies plus plates, placemats, and napkins on a tray. She puts the tray down, gives CHRISTINE the plate of cookies, and returns to setting the table.

JULIE: Did he disrupt the system?

MARK: Yes! They stood in his honour!

JULIE: The guy told his daughter that the man in charge of *that lynching* had a "blind spot"!

MARK: So?!

JULIE: That the head of the lynch mob was basically a good guy with—I'm sorry, that's ableist.

CHRISTINE: Yeah, you can't say blind spot. I was going to tell you.

JULIE: Thanks. Sorry.

MARK: Atticus was about turning the other cheek.

JULIE: Sorry, I was ableist.

(to herself) I messed up. I'm so sorry. No excuses!

MARK: Hello?

JULIE: I can't believe I said that.

CHRISTINE: It's okay.

JULIE: No, it isn't. And then you say the phrase? You didn't have to say the phrase to tell me I shouldn't say the phrase!

CHRISTINE: That's true, actually. / When you're right, you're right.

MARK: Hello! Harper Lee didn't know that "blind spot" was ableist! I didn't even know that was ableist till now! Oh my God!

PRECY: Mark, ito nanaman nag mumura ka / ulit!

MARK: Sorry, Precy!

PRECY: *(to herself)* It's like I'm not here today!

CHRISTINE: *(to MARK)* I didn't know / either.

MARK: *(smiling)* I'm sorry, Precy. You know I'm sorry.

(to JULIE) Atticus Finch is my personal hero.

CHRISTINE: I didn't know this. Why wouldn't you tell me this?

MARK: Atticus Finch was as godly as you could get back then.

JULIE: But he wasn't. He basically told Scout that lynching a Black man was simply an awareness issue?

MARK: I'm not making light of the seriousness here, but Scout was a child.

JULIE: Exactly. How do we teach children about this kind of hatred?

MARK: For the win! Compare and contrast the 1930s to today. Ding / ding.

JULIE: The 1930s to today . . .

MARK: Feels good to learn from me, doesn't it? Party finish.

JULIE: No. Nope. Round three. Back up, back up . . . It's coming to me now . . . I got it . . . I got it . . . Okay. Boo Radley. Weird, scary white man. Saved Jem by killing the town racist. Not brought into court. No trial. Scout walks him home, safe and sound. The police protected him. *That* still happens today. The Privilege.

MARK: No one was talking about privilege back then.

CHRISTINE cozies up to MARK.

JULIE: Tom Robinson. An innocent Black disabled man—

MARK: No one used the word privileged back then.

JULIE: Was shot seventeen times—

MARK: White privilege—that word was created what, in 1980? 1984?

He looks at CHRISTINE. She doesn't want to get involved.

Like . . .

JULIE: Tom Robinson was shot seventeen times, unarmed, running from the cops. Seventeen times!

CHRISTINE: Really?

JULIE: You didn't read that part?

CHRISTINE: I did. I just didn't . . .

JULIE: Seventeen times.

> MARK *has stopped listening to them and is reading the treatment. When* PRECY *has finished setting the table, she returns to the kitchen. She puts five juice glasses on a tray.*

The book doesn't encourage people to stop racism when they see it. The moment it happens . . . Wow . . . It's gotta be the nostalgia, I think . . . This book, the film, makes people feel good. Like you, Mark. Yeah . . . it must be nostalgia . . . You feel so good, you don't even see the problem.

(*to* MARK) You need an anti-oppression workshop.

MARK: . . .

JULIE: Both of you actually need to take an anti-oppression workshop.

CHRISTINE: I would totally take an anti-oppression workshop!

MARK: I'm the one who told my firm we needed diversity training.

JULIE: You literally cannot—

MARK: And we got diversity training.

JULIE: You cannot see—

MARK: What I *can* see is that you've added Indigenous characters to your treatment.

JULIE: (*to* MARK) Yes.

MARK: There were zero Indigenous characters in the novel.

JULIE: So?

MARK: How are you writing about Indigenous people?

JULIE: There were Indigenous people in America during that time.

MARK: You aren't Indigenous.

JULIE: Colonized land.

MARK: Okay.

JULIE: We are on *colonized land*.

MARK: Okay.

JULIE: We are migrants. The Finches are settlers. We are on colonized land.

MARK: Okay. Okay.

JULIE: It's interconnected. It is all interconnected.

MARK: You didn't create racism. So why do you think you have to solve it?

   Silence.

It's a Pulitzer Prize–winning book. It's taught in schools.

JULIE: So?

MARK: It's iconic. *The film is iconic.*

JULIE: Zero fucks—

MARK: Dad got you a Hollywood agent and you're blowing it.

JULIE: *Zero fucks—*

MARK: You represent our family and you're blowing it.

JULIE: *Zero. Fucks. Given.*

    LAWRENCE enters.

LAWRENCE: It's a little cold out there, so grab your jackets.

MARK: He cancelled?

LAWRENCE: He was double-checking the address and wanted to know about wine. Game plan. We start with the article. He hasn't read it. I told him about it, but hasn't read it.

MARK: (*to LAWRENCE*) Is that how you're gonna get her film produced, because you always make things happen for her?

(*to JULIE*) You're going to fail and take us all down with you.

JULIE: Anyone want to step in?

MARK: Do you know how bad this will be for my career?

JULIE: Because . . .

MARK: I wasn't kidding when I said write about Dad!

JULIE: You're a fraud! You know you're a fraud!

LAWRENCE: Let's take a breath.

MARK exits. PRECY enters and sets glasses on the table.

How's that hot water, Christine?

CHRISTINE: Good, Mr. Gordon. Almost . . . almost done.

LAWRENCE: Don't forget to put your cup in the dishwasher.

CHRISTINE: Sorry?

LAWRENCE nods his head in JULIE's direction, which JULIE doesn't see, and physically indicates to CHRISTINE to cheer JULIE up. Then—

LAWRENCE: Cup. Dishwasher.

LAWRENCE gives CHRISTINE a final look and gesture. CHRISTINE understands LAWRENCE's code. LAWRENCE exits. When PRECY has finished setting the glasses, she returns to the kitchen.

CHRISTINE: I get what you're saying. Write the screenplay.

JULIE nods.

It's more realistic.

JULIE continues nodding.

It's feminist!

JULIE continues.

It's political. Black housekeepers. We don't know enough about them.

JULIE: Yes! Portrayed to be lazy and mean and angry but then are the most hard-working group of women on the globe!

CHRISTINE: We keep studying *old stories* about whiteness and white privilege. Like, are there no other books?

JULIE looks at her. Beat.

Are you sure you don't want to come to St. Barts? Your treat last year! My treat this year!

JULIE: . . .

CHRISTINE: Please come with me.

JULIE: . . .

CHRISTINE: I'm not ditching these tickets.

JULIE: . . .

CHRISTINE: I miss you! It's been so long since we—this is what we do, we honour our moms this way. We've done it for years, this is about our *moms*. We do this *together*. You can write in the hotel, please come.

LAWRENCE enters.

JULIE: I don't know.

Silence. CHRISTINE enters the kitchen, teary-eyed. She blows her nose.

CHRISTINE: Precy, if Mark is looking for me, just tell him I went to the bathroom, okay?

PRECY: Okay.

CHRISTINE gives LAWRENCE a look and then exits. As LAWRENCE exits, he indicates that PRECY should join him. PRECY does. Alone, JULIE closes her laptop and takes some space.

JULIE: *(to GLORIA)* Help me find my voice? Please?

JULIE sprawls out on the ground. LAWRENCE re-enters.

LAWRENCE: We're going to be out of your hair in no time.

JULIE: Thanks.

Beat.

I'm feeling like I want to quit this.

LAWRENCE: . . .

JULIE: Like . . . I can't write this.

LAWRENCE sits with JULIE.

LAWRENCE: Sweetheart, you're a writer. You have an agent. You can do this.

JULIE: You got me that agent.

LAWRENCE: And?

JULIE: And? I didn't get it by myself! And Mark! He didn't either!

LAWRENCE: Mmmhm.

JULIE: Ughhhhhh . . . They make me feel like I'm back in university. I put all that time into my pitch and I failed. I was on the spot. I shouldn't have to explain why Calpurnia . . . Like, everywhere I turn, I have to explain why my writing is believable, Black women overcome the odds, the obstacles—

> PRECY *enters the kitchen. She cleans and gets organized. She puts five wine glasses and cutlery on a tray.*

That prof would not believe that a Black woman from Jamaica could be a doctor during the seventies. That Mom should be a nurse. Like I was lying about Mom being a doctor.

LAWRENCE: You're not in university, love.

JULIE: He has a stereotype burned in his mind. And when I do write the truth, no one believes it.

LAWRENCE: And what did you do?

JULIE: . . .

LAWRENCE: What did you do?

JULIE: I wrote it anyway.

LAWRENCE: And?

JULIE: My class loved it.

LAWRENCE: And?

JULIE: I don't know. I barely passed the class?

LAWRENCE: And?

JULIE: I fought for my grade. Is this life? If you don't put it in my lap, is the next step always a fight? What if I'm just bad at everything?

LAWRENCE: Hard when the past creeps up on you.

JULIE: Maybe I'm nothing without your help? I can't write Black people.

Silence.

He said Black people don't talk like that.

Silence.

He doesn't think I have a Black voice. He basically said I'm not Black enough to write this movie. What if he's . . .

LAWRENCE: Impossible.

JULIE: What if Mom's not proud of me?

LAWRENCE: . . .

JULIE: She doesn't know me.

LAWRENCE: . . .

JULIE: What will I—?

Silence.

LAWRENCE: I don't know how writers do it, but you do. Do whatever you need to do. Get *in there*—how she speaks, who she is. You have the whole afternoon. Do what you need to do and then eat with us tonight.

Don't let the ignorance keep you down. And don't let it burn you to a crisp either. Mummy knows exactly who you are. Mummy . . .

They hug. Silence.

Help me get your brother into a new firm?

Meghan Swaby as Julie and Andrew Moodie as Lawrence. Produced by Nightwood Theatre and Sulong Theatre. Set Design: Anna Treusch, Costume Design: Jackie Chau, Lighting Design: Bonnie Beecher. Photo by Dahlia Katz.

JULIE: Fine. Yes.

(*snarky*) I'll help you get my brother into one of the most prestigious law firms in Toronto.

LAWRENCE: Excellent. Thank you. You're going to finish this.

> *He kisses her on the cheek.* LAWRENCE *walks towards the hall closet and pulls out three biking helmets.*

(*calling*) Hurry up, you two!

(*to* JULIE, *hugging her*) I gotta find you a main squeeze.

JULIE: Don't say main squeeze.

LAWRENCE: A shorty. A girlfriend. A theybee. / Boo?

JULIE: A they / . . . bee?

LAWRENCE: *A boo?* A bae. A beebee.

JULIE: Yeah, no, don't say any of those things.

LAWRENCE: A snuggle muffin?

LAWRENCE hugs her again.

(*calling*) I'm in the garage! You have five minutes!

(*to PRECY, singing*) There will be lumpia tonight! There will be lumpia tonight!

As he sings, he does a little dance with PRECY. She dances along.

PRECY: Yes, Mr. Gordon.

LAWRENCE exits with a helmet.

Because time grows on trees!

(*to JULIE*) Too much swearing, eh! It's Sunday. Mag respecto kayo sa akin dito sa itong Bahay nito! Ano ba?

JULIE: Yep. I apologize. Sorry.

PRECY: You can do whatever you want. Just no swearing.

JULIE: Okay.

PRECY: You promise?

JULIE: Yep.

PRECY: (*re: the wine glasses*) Oh!

PRECY continues her work. JULIE reads MARK's article in silence. MARK and CHRISTINE enter, wearing matching outfits. MARK goes to pick up the two helmets.

Killer article!

MARK: Thanks.

JULIE: They wrote some really nice things about you.

MARK: Yeah, they did.

JULIE: You'll get into the firm.

MARK: You think so?

JULIE: Yeah, you'll—

MARK: You know what?

CHRISTINE: Don't do it.

MARK: As a member of this family, I have a huge problem with what you're writing about.

PRECY: Oooo ito na.

JULIE: Hey, don't worry about it. My next screenplay will definitely be about Dad. / Definitely.

MARK: No. This is an embarrassment. You believe that you can write a screenplay about a poor, Black, lower-class, uneducated African American woman—living in the Deep South during the Depression. You're rich! You've never worked a day in your life! Think about where you live! The only Black men you know are Dad and me! You don't even visit our family in Jamaica! You don't even have Black

Matthew Brown as Mark and Natasha Greenblatt as Christine. Produced by Nightwood Theatre and Sulong Theatre. Set Design: Anna Treusch, Costume Design: Jackie Chau, Lighting Design: Bonnie Beecher. Photo by Dahlia Katz.

friends! If your agent tells you that you can't find the voice? You're not Black enough!

CHRISTINE: Mark.

MARK: (*in patois*) No!

(*to CHRISTINE*) She not!

(*to JULIE*) Yu not!

> MARK *exits.*

CHRISTINE: He's pissed.

> CHRISTINE *picks up two bicycle helmets from the armchair. Silence.*

Uh . . . I know this isn't the right time, but please please think about the trip, okay? Okay, see you in a bit. Precy . . . Are we having those little egg rolls?

PRECY: *(whispers)* I'll make you extra lumpia to take home.

CHRISTINE: Eeee! Yes, lumpia, of course, I'm— Okay! Bye, Lee Lee!

CHRISTINE *exits.* JULIE *is ordering an Uber on her phone.*

PRECY: Julie . . . Are you okay?

JULIE: Nope.

PRECY: So rude what he said. You want me to phone him? I will phone—

JULIE: No, no. Dad's thinking I should get into it, so can you help me, please? I know you're busy. But . . . Can I interview you now?

PRECY: You don't want me to read the book first?

JULIE *starts to record* PRECY *on her cellphone.* PRECY *is nervous.*

JULIE: I'm recording you, all good?

PRECY: Okay, but—how will I sound?

JULIE: It's just me listening. Don't worry about it.

PRECY: Ha ha! Okay.

JULIE: What does it feel like to be a housekeeper?

PRECY: Whaat? Are we starting?

JULIE: Yes.

PRECY: AHH!

JULIE: How does it feel? Uh. I'm sorry. He's right. I can't do this.

PRECY: He's just being mean. It's just a bad mood. Time to start—time to start.

JULIE: I—

JULIE is emotional.

PRECY: Shh . . . shh . . . shh . . .

(*whispers*) It's okay, it's okay . . . Begin again. What do you want to say?

JULIE: Uhhhh . . . Okay . . . first? The issues that Black women face? Not the same issues that Filipino women face, yeah?

Pause.

PRECY: . . . Would you like some ubas?

JULIE: Thanks! Yes. Just saying it's not the same because I'm asking you a bunch of questions about work.

PRECY: Okay.

Beat.

I have family in California—they are housekeepers—you want to talk to them?

JULIE: Maybe. Later? My Uber will be here.

PRECY: But you know, Julie, we are all people. We all bleed the same blood.

JULIE: But . . . Things are different for Black maids, servants, butlers, domestics . . .

PRECY: Then why interview *me*?

JULIE: Uh . . . Right . . . I'm just going to focus on your work. Not race. Okay?

> PRECY *brings the ubas to* JULIE. JULIE's *in a rush.*

My Uber's close. Speak from your gut. What does it feel like to be a housekeeper?

PRECY: It feels fine. Like a job. Some days are good days. Some days are bad.

JULIE: Do you *like* being a housekeeper?

PRECY: *(re: the wine glasses)* Oh!

> *She takes the tray of wine glasses and puts them on the table.*

Yes.

JULIE: Do you wish you could be something else?

PRECY: I would love to be a movie star!

JULIE: . . .

PRECY: I *love* what I do.

JULIE: But . . . What do you really *wish* you could do?

PRECY: Well, I would love to go for vacation.

JULIE: Where would you go?

PRECY: The Philippines.

JULIE: You're *from* the Philippines.

PRECY: I *love* the Philippines.

JULIE: You were just there. For like a month.

PRECY: So?

JULIE: Are we talking resort vacation or . . .

> *PRECY cleans up the plate of cookies and JULIE's mug from the living room. JULIE follows her around.*

PRECY: Yes. I go on resort vacations in the Philippines. Because I love the Philippines. I take my husband, my girls. They love it back home, so they choose to stay there. My granddaughters are in private school! So smart.

JULIE: For the record, you're the youngest grandmother I know. How old were you when they were—

PRECY: Asian don't raisin.

JULIE: . . .

PRECY: Raisin. Wrinkle. Heard that on the TV. And, hello, don't ask my age! On record, pa?! Rushing—rushing! Ay!

JULIE: I have to! You go to church with your friends?

PRECY: Of course! My friends, they all work around here, some lolas, some ates. All of them have children back home, except for one.

JULIE: All your friends are maids?

PRECY: Housekeepers. Most of them. Most work around here, but all over. I love my church.

JULIE: So—

PRECY: "Thou shalt love thy neighbour as thyself. There is none other commandment greater than this."

JULIE: Press?

PRECY: Mark 12:31. Last week's service— Oooo, you know who needs Mark 12? Mark needs Mark 12.

JULIE: Great. What else?

PRECY: (*panicked*) Julie!

JULIE: What?!

PRECY: I have to start the lumpia!!!!

JULIE: Yes, I know but—

PRECY: I have to go buy!

(*mutters, to herself*) What do I have at home?

JULIE: Uh . . . How much money do you make?

PRECY: (*offended*) Excuse me! None of your business! I am paid well. Very, very well.

JULIE: Did you always wear that?

PRECY: This is my uniform!

JULIE: What does it feel like *to serve*?

PRECY: I don't really *serve*!

JULIE: But . . . what does it *feel like* to be . . . like a *servant*?

PRECY: I'm not a *servant*, Julie!

JULIE stops recording.

JULIE: I know. I know. You're not. Sorry. For the research. Precy. Thank you!

She responds to a message on her phone.

I have to go.

PRECY: What?! That's it? What about—?

JULIE: I have an idea.

She gathers her things.

I will be back for dinner.

She gets her coat.

Thanks again, Precy. So helpful. There's my Uber! Gotta go!

She runs out the main door.

PRECY: Ay nako! Black people!

End of Act One.

INTERLUDE

*PRECY enters. She briskly puts the treatment and books on top
of the laptop. She takes the laptop, treatment, and books to
the table with the urn sitting on top and places them on a shelf
below the urn.*

*She returns to the dinner table and takes the fifth placemat,
plates, and cutlery from the table. She arranges the setting at
the head of the table.*

*She returns to the kitchen. She picks up the clothes on the
chair. Then she exits to the second kitchen, where the roast is
being made.*

*As PRECY exits, MARK and CHRISTINE enter playfully. They dump
their bike helmets on one of the armchairs. They continue to be
flirtatious and playful.*

*PRECY enters with the roast beef in a casserole dish. She places it
on the kitchen island and then opens the oven door. Then she
puts the roast beef in the oven.*

*As MARK and CHRISTINE exit, PRECY fills the ice bucket with a lot of
ice. She picks up the bucket and crosses to the bar cart, placing it
on top. She goes to pick up the helmets off the comfy chair.*

*As she picks them up, LAWRENCE enters through the main
entrance—helmet in hand. PRECY takes his helmet and puts all
three helmets away in the closet.*

He stops to look at Gloria's portrait. LAWRENCE *and* PRECY *have a shared moment as they both look at her.*

Then, LAWRENCE *quickly exits.* PRECY *goes to the closet to get her jacket and scarf. She puts them on. She enters the kitchen and then exits through the back door.*

JULIE *enters from the front door with a Popeyes bag and an unmarked clothing bag. She sees* PRECY *exit but* PRECY *doesn't see her.*

As JULIE *passes the side tables, she sees* MARK's *articles. She picks them up and puts them in the recycling bin.*

She quickly walks into the kitchen, opens a lower cupboard, and places the Popeyes inside. She exits to her bedroom.

As JULIE *exits,* PRECY *enters.* PRECY *doesn't see* JULIE. PRECY *sets fresh flowers and a Tupperware container of lumpia down on the kitchen island.*

PRECY *checks the oven and inhales the scent from her delicious food. She goes to the garbage can, pulls out the garbage, and exits the kitchen through the back door. She throws out the garbage and puts on her blazer.*

ACT TWO

MARK enters. He walks into the kitchen, finds the lumpia, and begins to emotionally eat.

CHRISTINE: *(entering, holding her heels)* Babyyyyyyy.

CHRISTINE brushes crumbs from MARK's blazer and makes sure he looks put together.

MARK: Do I want this too much? I feel needy. Am I coming off needy?

LAWRENCE enters.

LAWRENCE: Where's Julie?

CHRISTINE: Knocked on her door, no answer.

Their long, classical doorbell chimes. They listen intently, holding their breath, standing completely still as the bell finishes ringing.

LAWRENCE: Where's Precy?

CHRISTINE attempts to fix LAWRENCE's blazer. It's awkward. He doesn't need it.

(calling) Julie!

MARK: Dad?

LAWRENCE: A grand night, a grand night, a grand night!

MARK: Where's Julie?

CHRISTINE: Deep breath, baby.

> *MARK checks his breath for the smell. He gargles water. He takes out chewing gum and chews it.*

LAWRENCE: (*calling*) Julie! She'll come down.

(*at the door*) Siri, play some dinner-party jazz.

> *Music plays. CHRISTINE puts on her heels. LAWRENCE leads MARK and CHRISTINE through a deep inhale and exhale. MARK takes out his gum to inhale and exhale. After they finish, CHRISTINE grabs MARK's hand and takes him to the door. They share a silent gum moment. CHRISTINE takes the gum. LAWRENCE opens the front door. James THOMPSON enters with a bottle of wine and a plant.*

THOMPSON: Lar / ry!

LAWRENCE: Thanks for / coming, James.

THOMPSON: Blazers both? / I

LAWRENCE: It's / oh (kay)

THOMPSON: I thought cas(ual) ah / hh

LAWRENCE: It's / oh (kay)

THOMPSON: I'm early! I hope that's— Beautiful home!

> *PRECY enters. She quickly washes her hands, realizing that she is late.*

LAWRENCE: Thank you.

THOMPSON: So much land.

LAWRENCE: Thank you.

THOMPSON: Gorgeous gardens!

LAWRENCE: This is Mark.

THOMPSON: Your lawn is outstanding. The ivy?

(to MARK) Yes, nice to finally meet you. And this is—

MARK: This is my girlfriend, Christine.

CHRISTINE: Nice to meet you, sir.

> *PRECY takes the bottle of wine from* THOMPSON. *PRECY drops it off in the kitchen.*

THOMPSON: Very nice to meet you. *(gives CHRISTINE the plant)* Larry, this property is just—! No damage with the ivy?

> *LAWRENCE takes the plant.*

LAWRENCE: None. No damage.

THOMPSON: None? What about the trees?

> *LAWRENCE gives PRECY the plant.*

LAWRENCE: We had them planted when the kids were born. No root damage? Is that what you're—

THOMPSON: But the ivy. The ivy!

LAWRENCE: Thank you. No root damage, no!

THOMPSON: I'm lucky I didn't bring Tonya.

LAWRENCE: Hey, I tried to talk her into coming.

THOMPSON: She'd have my head! I told her we couldn't have ivy.

LAWRENCE: Care for a drink?

> PRECY *goes to the bar cart.*

(*friendly*) Thanks, Precy.

> PRECY *heads to the kitchen and starts working.*

(*to* THOMPSON) Is Tonya okay?

MARK: I can make a drink!

THOMPSON: Sure.

(*to* LAWRENCE) Can't stay too long.

LAWRENCE: (*friendly*) Thanks, Precy.

(*to* THOMPSON) Is Tonya okay?

THOMPSON: Yeah, she's at home with the girls.

LAWRENCE: She could've come.

THOMPSON: She's fine. Work's work.

LAWRENCE: Thanks for coming.

THOMPSON: Oh, no, no, no. It's quite all right. Maybe the number of the landscaping company!

THOMPSON, LAWRENCE, and MARK laugh.

That'd be fine. Kidding, kidding, kidding.

LAWRENCE: We won't keep you too long. And I'd love . . .

JULIE hums from upstairs.

I'd love to give you our landscaper's number.

THOMPSON: But honestly. It's incredible out there! This is exactly how we wanted our front lawn.

LAWRENCE: We had the whole place built about thirty years ago.

MARK: What would you like to drink, Mr. Thompson?

THOMPSON: James is fine. Appletons.

LAWRENCE: I'll have one too. Christine, you want to grab the album?

CHRISTINE looks at MARK. MARK points to where the album is kept. She gets the album.

Documented the entire build. My wife and I would drive back and forth.

LAWRENCE puts his hand out to take THOMPSON's jacket.

THOMPSON: Thank you.

THOMPSON takes off his jacket.

I honestly don't think that we're going to have a summer this year. It should be a lot warmer outside.

> JULIE *enters in full Southern maid garb—skirt, apron, shirt, head tie, and a red towel hangs from her apron tie. The anxiety in the room ramps up.* THOMPSON *is open to the new experience.*

JULIE: Excuse me, Lawrence. Sorry, Mr. Mark. I's runnin' behind all day. Been cookin' and cleanin'.

(*re: the jacket*) I'll take that.

> JULIE *takes* THOMPSON'*s jacket.* MARK *goes to pull it away from her.* JULIE *has a grip on it, so they are both holding it tightly.*

Mr. Mark, don't you give me no trouble now. Jus' tryin' to hang up the man's coat!

(*to* THOMPSON) Evenin', suh.

> JULIE *curtsies.* JULIE *and* MARK *struggle with the jacket.*

LAWRENCE: My daughter. Julie. Writing a screenplay about *To Kill a Mockingbird.*

THOMPSON: Outstanding! When's it coming out?

> JULIE *and* MARK *are in a standoff. Awkward silence.* PRECY *arrives and grabs the jacket.*

LAWRENCE: Yes. And obviously she's in character . . . trying to gain some inspiration . . .

> MARK *grabs* JULIE *by the arm and takes her into the kitchen. She grabs an article she missed earlier, which* MARK *doesn't see, and puts it in the recycling bin as* MARK *pulls her off stage.*

JULIE: (*crossing*) *Oh, Mister Gordon*! I's sorry!

PRECY hangs the jacket in the closet, then goes to the kitchen to prepare the lemonade.

LAWRENCE: She's having some writer's block and she's just . . . trying to clear her head . . . get some ideas . . .

THOMPSON: Interesting. Like method acting? Marlon Brando, that sort of thing.

LAWRENCE is distracted. JULIE wails off stage.

Marlon . . . Brando . . .

LAWRENCE: Yes . . . I . . . Earlier . . . we were talking . . . about reflecting on . . . a maid's . . . point of . . . view and . . . researching that point of . . . view . . . so . . .

THOMPSON: Oh.

LAWRENCE: Doing whatever you can to get to the . . . heart . . . of the . . . character . . .

THOMPSON admires some art.

THOMPSON: Oh! Fine by me.

(*to LAWRENCE*) You heard of Basquiat?

LAWRENCE is distracted.

CHRISTINE: I love Basquiat!

THOMPSON: As long as I'm home on time, everything is a-okay.

Andrew Moodie as Lawrence and Don Allison as Thompson. Produced by Nightwood Theatre and Sulong Theatre. Set Design: Anna Treusch, Costume Design: Jackie Chau, Lighting Design: Bonnie Beecher. Photo by Dahlia Katz.

LAWRENCE: Thank you.

THOMPSON: Tonya will be staring down the clock.

LAWRENCE: Home on time. Early, in fact.

JULIE: (*off stage*) Please, Mr. Mark!

THOMPSON: Julie an . . . actor?

LAWRENCE: No.

THOMPSON: Oh. I was thinking maybe she was one of those method actors. You know, get into the role, live the role.

LAWRENCE: No, she's . . . a writer.

THOMPSON: I see. University project?

LAWRENCE: No. She just graduated. She's with a big-time literary agent, the world's leading entertainment agency, and she needs to do some character work . . . She got a—got a few notes about the character's "voice" so . . . She's just . . . researching? Wouldn't you say that, Christine?

JULIE enters. She tastes the lemonade and then adds sugar to it, all while PRECY has her back turned.

CHRISTINE: Yeah, researching. She's . . . researching Black maids in the 1930s . . . *getting into the role.* That's normal. Tons of artists do it. Would you like to look at the album, sir?

THOMPSON: James.

CHRISTINE: I can make a drink, Mr. Gordon.

LAWRENCE: Yes, Christine. Thank you.

JULIE stirs the lemonade with a large serving spoon. CHRISTINE makes two drinks. LAWRENCE shows THOMPSON photographs of the massive renovation.

MARK: Stop.

JULIE: Suh.

MARK: Julie.

JULIE: Mah name's Calpurnia, suh.

MARK: Go upstairs, put yourself together properly!

JULIE: Mr. Mark. I'm gonna have to ask you to not touch me like that ever again. I know my rights. And I am *not* afraid to cry out.

PRECY: Oy.

MARK: Don't.

JULIE: Mr. Marcus. I know my rights. I've been in this home from the day you were born. Changed those diapers before you knew what to do in them.

MARK: Stop this!

JULIE: *I will cry out.* I am here to serve and I'm gonna do it well.

MARK and JULIE tussle. JULIE wins.

I'll serve naked, sir. This my job.

LAWRENCE: Everything all right, Mark?

MARK: *(shaken)* Yes, Dad.

LAWRENCE: Wonderful. I'm just showing James here what the house looked like before you and Julie were born.

MARK: Oh yeah?

LAWRENCE: You know, he's seen this book so many times. Come. Sit with—

MARK sits. PRECY picks up the tray of lemonade and enters the living room. JULIE follows her and takes the tray from her. They stand beside each other. CHRISTINE serves THOMPSON and LAWRENCE their drinks.

THOMPSON: So . . . Mark . . . Congratulations!

MARK: Thanks, sir.

THOMPSON: Your dad told me about your interview in the paper. This early in your career? It's going to bring you loads of work.

MARK: Thank you, sir.

THOMPSON: I'm impressed.

MARK: Thanks. I had no clue I was even being watched.

THOMPSON: You're always being watched.

CHRISTINE looks at MARK.

MARK: Ha ha. I guess.

JULIE: *(to all)* Lemonade, suhs.

LAWRENCE: *(to THOMPSON)* After you.

Rochelle Kives as Precy, Kwaku Adu-Poku as Mark, Emerjade Simms as Julie, Arne MacPherson as Thompson, Ellie Ellwand as Christine, and Ray Strachan as Lawrence. Produced by the National Arts Centre, the Royal Manitoba Theatre Centre, and Black Theatre Workshop. Set Design: Rachel Forbes, Costume Design: Joseph Abetria, Lighting Design: Hugh Conacher. Photo by Dylan Hewlett.

JULIE presents the tray of lemonade to THOMPSON. *She bows before him.*

THOMPSON: Thank you.

He sips.

Freshly squeezed. A little . . . sugary.

JULIE: I'm sorry, suh. I kin—

LAWRENCE: Never mind, Julie.

JULIE: Calpurnia . . . suh.

JULIE offers MARK *a glass. He goes to take it. She tricks him and pulls it away before he can grasp it.*

(*to* MARK) Too sweet for tha sweet.

JULIE exits into the kitchen.

THOMPSON: (*laughing*) She's not making the meal, is she?

MARK *laughs nervously.*

LAWRENCE: Oh God no. Precy has made us a wonderful meal.

PRECY: Yes, sir. It is delicious. Very very delicious.

THOMPSON: Starving. I left my wife cooking ackee . . . salt fish . . .

CHRISTINE: Your wife was cooking on Mother's Day?

THOMPSON: She loves cooking. I'm not going to stop her. And we don't ask our housekeeper to work on Sundays.

PRECY: *(lying)* I love working on Sundays! Let me get you some hors d'oeuvres. You must be hungry.

PRECY returns to the kitchen.

LAWRENCE: Can I top you up?

CHRISTINE takes THOMPSON's drink out of his hand.

THOMPSON: Oh! Okay. Where's this article, I'd love to read / it—

MARK: I'll—

MARK doesn't see the newspapers where he left them.

THOMPSON: The . . . article?

LAWRENCE scans the room for the article.

MARK: I'll be . . . right back.

CHRISTINE: Getting ice!

MARK exits. CHRISTINE leaves THOMPSON's drink on the bar cart. She enters the kitchen with the ice bucket, which is already filled with ice. LAWRENCE looks up the article on his phone and gives his phone to THOMPSON.

PRECY: You added sugar to my lemonade?

JULIE: Uh . . . Too tart, honey. Mens love shugah!

PRECY: Here. Let me do it!

JULIE pours out some of the lemonade and starts to add water to it. PRECY prepares the main courses.

CHRISTINE: You have to stop this.

JULIE: Miss Christine. If you hungry, you just gonna have to wait.

CHRISTINE: . . .

JULIE: Making the lemonade right tasty, Miss Christine. One second!

CHRISTINE exits, still holding the ice bucket.

CHRISTINE: There is some magic happening in there! I think we're having roast. Do you like roast, James?

THOMPSON: Yeah, roast is fine. (*to LAWRENCE*) You been to Aunt Mary's Fish / Shack?

LAWRENCE shakes his head no.

The real thing. Fry fish, bammy, jerk.

LAWRENCE smiles and nods.

We'll go with Tonya. She'd love that.

PRECY brings out salt and pepper for the table.

PRECY: (*to CHRISTINE*) You need anything?

CHRISTINE: No.

THOMPSON: (*to CHRISTINE*) You?

CHRISTINE: No, I—

PRECY takes the ice bucket and returns it to its original place. She returns to the kitchen.

—but I'd *love* to.

THOMPSON: You cook.

CHRISTINE: I have a few dishes that I like to make.

MARK enters. He is overwhelmed.

MARK: (*to LAWRENCE, desperate*) I can't find the article!

THOMPSON: That's all right.

MARK: I can send you a link!

THOMPSON: Read it on your dad's phone. Ever been to Aunt Mary's?

JULIE retrieves the article and places it back on the side table. She returns to the kitchen.

MARK: Love Aunt Mary's.

THOMPSON: The fry fish?

MARK: The best.

THOMPSON: Ackee and salt fish?

MARK: Favourite place to get it.

CHRISTINE: Why haven't I been there?

THOMPSON: We're all going to go one of these days. I'll bring Tonya and the girls. It'll be great.

MARK: (*to* LAWRENCE) Should we talk about the article?

THOMPSON: Superb read. You've got a bright future.

LAWRENCE: You were in court on Friday.

MARK: Uhhh, sure! I . . . Friday . . .

> LAWRENCE *gives* MARK *a moment. Then—*

LAWRENCE: This one is tricky. All things considered. We have a long-term relationship between two young adults. Drug addicts. They are high and—

MARK: My client is being tried for sexual assault and physical assault.

LAWRENCE: Mark identifies problem areas for clients very well. He's good at research, at—

MARK: Thanks! So, my client is guilty. We know this.

THOMPSON: Black man? White man?

> PRECY *brings water glasses and a pitcher to the table. She pours water into the glasses.* JULIE *quickly begins to dish up the Popeyes and stashes it back in the cupboard.*

MARK: Black man. And his girlfriend, the woman he "allegedly assaulted," is on the stand. She's Polish.

LAWRENCE: She's also high. Make that crystal clear.

THOMPSON: So she can't remember what happened that night.

MARK: Yeah, exactly. When I ask her about the evening—

LAWRENCE: She can't remember!

(*to* THOMPSON) You've been there.

THOMPSON: You're not saying anything I haven't heard before!

MARK: Yeah, so she begins to backtrack.

THOMPSON: Backtrack.

MARK: Yeah. And I said to her, "Take your time. Try to remember. We have all of the time in the world."

THOMPSON: But you don't.

LAWRENCE: He knows that.

> THOMPSON *and* LAWRENCE *laugh* MARK *joins in.*

MARK: No, I don't. I mean, I know—I don't, have all of . . . all the—I know I don't have all the time in the world.

> CHRISTINE *laughs in support.*

THOMPSON: You made her feel relaxed?

MARK: Yeah.

THOMPSON: Didn't go for the jugular? Roar!

MARK: No, no, not my style, I guess.

THOMPSON: Nice guy?

MARK: She was *very, very* stressed.

THOMPSON: (*to* CHRISTINE) You got a nice boyfriend. Ha!

CHRISTINE: Yeah, he's very—

THOMPSON: I wasn't nice as a young lawyer. Were you?

LAWRENCE: Can't remember!

THOMPSON: (*friendly, to* LAWRENCE) So, born in Jamaica?

LAWRENCE: Yes.

THOMPSON: From yard?

LAWRENCE: No. Cherry Gardens.

THOMPSON: (*to* MARK) You're from here.

MARK *smiles and nods.*

(*to* LAWRENCE) You came up here when you were . . .

LAWRENCE: Three.

THOMPSON: Oh, so you weren't raised there?

LAWRENCE: No.

PRECY *brings out a bowl of horseradish and sets it on the table. She hovers over* THOMPSON.

Precy, you know you don't have to wait. You can go.

PRECY *returns to the kitchen. She prepares the main courses.*

THOMPSON: Siblings?

LAWRENCE: Only child.

THOMPSON: My wife, born in Mandeville. Family of fourteen. Her father, Old Johnson Mountain. Family of sixteen.

LAWRENCE: . . . Another?

THOMPSON: Appletons?

LAWRENCE: Estate 30.

THOMPSON: Oooo.

They laugh and LAWRENCE *makes* THOMPSON *a drink.*

Tonya's family came up in her teens.

LAWRENCE: A few families came up around the time my parents did.

THOMPSON: (*to* LAWRENCE) That'll do.

LAWRENCE *stops making* THOMPSON's *drink.*

Where'd you go to school?

LAWRENCE: Private school on—

MARK *walks to the kitchen.* JULIE *opens the fridge and takes out a salad bowl filled with salad.*

CHRISTINE: Mark, Julie, and I went to the same schools growing up. They were pretty multicultural.

THOMPSON: Private school?

CHRISTINE: Yeah.

MARK: Supper's okay?

PRECY: Yes, Mark. Everything is fine.

JULIE: Yes, suh! Served in a few!

PRECY: I don't talk like that!

> MARK *enters the living room.* PRECY *pulls out a tray of hors d'oeuvres and heads to the living room.* JULIE *pulls out the dish of popcorn chicken, sweet and sour sauce, and some napkins.* LAWRENCE *hands* THOMPSON *his drink.*

THOMPSON: You miss Jamaica?

LAWRENCE: Not—uh—

THOMPSON: The sand. The *spicy food.*

LAWRENCE: Too busy.

THOMPSON: You go back?

LAWRENCE: Wellll . . .

> LAWRENCE *shakes his head no, laughs.*

THOMPSON: How about you, son?

MARK: Uh . . . Last month.

THOMPSON: My wife and I? We go two, three times a year. Mandeville?

MARK: I've gone through it.

THOMPSON: (*to LAWRENCE*) You?

LAWRENCE: No.

THOMPSON: Tonya's from Mandeville.

MARK: I usually start at Grandpa's place in Cherry Gardens and then do my thing.

THOMPSON: Your thing?

MARK: Yeah, visit family, hike, hang out.

THOMPSON: Hang out? The bar?

MARK: Ha ha! Sometimes! I golf!

They laugh. JULIE enters with her dish.

THOMPSON: Golfing's good. You didn't tell me he golfed.

MARK: Beautiful greens in Jamaica! You have to see our grandpa's place! It is a quick drive from the—

JULIE: Pardon me, suh.

PRECY holds her tray out to THOMPSON.

PRECY: Sir.

JULIE holds her dish out to THOMPSON with a little more force.

JULIE: Suh.

Arne MacPherson as Thompson, Ellie Ellwand as Christine, Ray Strachan as Lawrence, Kwaku Adu-Poku as Mark, and Emerjade Simms as Julie. Produced by the National Arts Centre, the Royal Manitoba Theatre Centre, and Black Theatre Workshop. Set Design: Rachel Forbes, Costume Design: Joseph Abetria, Lighting Design: Hugh Conacher. Photo by Dylan Hewlett.

THOMPSON *takes a napkin and a piece of popcorn chicken. He dips the chicken in the sauce and eats.* THOMPSON *spits the chicken out into the napkin.*

Oh! Uh . . . Bad batch.

JULIE *exits.* THOMPSON *laughs. Everyone laughs.* JULIE *nearly trips.* MARK *goes to her. Everyone gasps.*

JULIE: I good!

JULIE *returns to the kitchen. She starts putting biscuits and coleslaw into bowls.* PRECY *puts appetizers back into the fridge.*

THOMPSON: (*to* MARK, *emotional*) Ever meet Dennis Tucker?

LAWRENCE: No.

THOMPSON: Best friend from law school. Came on board when his mom got sick. Had to hire him. No one else would back then. One day, he just dropped. Heart attack. He passed before his mom did.

MARK: My / condolences.

LAWRENCE: Sorry to hear.

THOMPSON: (*getting emotional*) Ahhh . . . Adored him. Agreeable. I'm all right, I'm all right. Good-hearted soul.

(*to MARK*) You two are . . . (so similar). Ahhh . . . sorry, sorry, and how long have you two been together?

MARK: Uhh . . .

THOMPSON: Not good. He should know that number.

CHRISTINE: Two years!   **LAWRENCE:** Two years!

THOMPSON: That's nice.

CHRISTINE: We live together.

THOMPSON: Is that so?

CHRISTINE: I've known the Gordons my entire life.

MARK: Christine's family's in oil.

THOMPSON: Your dad?

CHRISTINE: Grandparents. Great-grandparents.

THOMPSON: Let me guess, you graduated with straight As . . . Women's Studies . . . And volunteer work!

CHRISTINE: Gender Studies, actually.

THOMPSON: Gender Studies.

CHRISTINE: I don't volunteer, but I do work with at-risk youth.

MARK: She was at the top of her class.

THOMPSON: Like you?

MARK: Yes.

CHRISTINE: My grades were better than yours, if we're going to . . .

MARK: She's younger, / competitive.

THOMPSON: Younger woman. I get it.

Off CHRISTINE's *look—*

MARK: You are.

CHRISTINE: Funnily enough, despite age, I am more adult and . . . someone he looks up to. Right? *Right*?

MARK: Yeah, yeah, yeah.

THOMPSON: Good couple.

CHRISTINE: I wouldn't trade Mark in for anything.

JULIE: I sure do hope not!

JULIE pours out lemonade, tasting it for sweetness and adding more water.

PRECY: *(re: the lemonade)* Let me try.

JULIE: No you will not.

JULIE enters the living room with lemonade.

CHRISTINE: I started a cycling initiative. We provide bikes and train youth for a race that happens every fall.

THOMPSON: At-risk youth? That's good.

JULIE: What they're at risk of, Lord knows I'll never know!

CHRISTINE: They learn about endurance, health, discipline, values.

JULIE: *(to CHRISTINE)* Here yuh go, Missus Charter!

JULIE hands her a glass of lemonade. They stand beside each other.

CHRISTINE: Teamwork.

She takes a sip.

Uhm. Yeah. Julie used to be *involved before she started writing . . .*

JULIE hums "Wade in the Water."

THOMPSON: *(warmly)* You snatched up a good one, Mark.

MARK: *(to THOMPSON)* Pardon me?

THOMPSON: Educated. Great values.

MARK: Thanks.

CHRISTINE gives JULIE back her lemonade. JULIE stops singing and goes back to the kitchen. She prepares her dishes.

THOMPSON: *(endearing)* Girls like her—*(kind)* you're very beautiful, miss—don't come along every three weeks, son.

(to CHRISTINE) You love this man?

CHRISTINE: Ha! Yes!

THOMPSON: You gotta propose, son.

LAWRENCE: I've been saying the same thing!

THOMPSON: *(winking)* She'll say yes.

THOMPSON stands.

My girls got married this February.

LAWRENCE: Both of them?

THOMPSON: Valentine's Day wedding. What a fight *that* was. The flowers. The dresses.

PRECY continues preparing the meal.

LAWRENCE: I can only imagine.

THOMPSON: The best part of the evening was the soca!

MARK: You like soca?

THOMPSON: It's all I listen to.

MARK: Dad hates it.

THOMPSON: What?!

LAWRENCE: Not my cup of tea.

THOMPSON: We love it. Only thing stopping us from having that wedding during Carnival was that the girls weren't into it and the grooms couldn't convince them.

MARK: Seriously?

THOMPSON: I couldn't believe it.

THOMPSON dances.

(*in patois*) It's in alla yu bones.

JULIE starts to hum "Wade in the Water" again.

(*to JULIE*) Ya! I like gospel too! Gospel's great! Son, you're not getting any younger. You're how old now?

MARK: Twenty-eight.

JULIE hums quieter.

THOMPSON: (*laughing*) Can't ask the lady her age! So . . .

CHRISTINE: It's fine! I'm in my— I'm in my younger, younger twenties so . . .

THOMPSON: You love this man?

CHRISTINE: Uh . . . yes, I do.

THOMPSON: Mark. You love this woman?

MARK: Yes. I . . . do.

THOMPSON: Well.

MARK: (*laughing*) I feel like I'm getting married.

    JULIE stops humming.

THOMPSON: You're a good kid.

LAWRENCE: He'll win his case.

THOMPSON: Easy win.

MARK: You think so?

THOMPSON: Well, between you and me, with confidence, you have won before you started.

(*to LAWRENCE*) How's that meal coming along?

    PRECY and JULIE speed up their work.

MARK: Ha! You're right.

LAWRENCE: It's easy for the young ones to feel doubtful.

(*loudly*) I think it will be here shortly.

THOMPSON: How's the girl on the stand though? She wasn't saying very much?

MARK: Yes, she was backtracking and—

THOMPSON: That can work for you.

MARK: Yes, well . . . she was so scared. She was speechless for a sec. I said to her, "Sounds like you need to take a deep breath." And then she did!

THOMPSON: You told her to take a deep breath?

MARK: Yeah.

THOMPSON: Am I in *Mister Rogers' Neighborhood*? You get the reference?

LAWRENCE: He gets the reference.

MARK: Yeah.

THOMPSON: Haha, okay, so what happened after she took a deep breath.

MARK: She cried.

THOMPSON: She cried? You made her cry?

LAWRENCE: Of course not!

MARK: No, I didn't make her cry. She was having a release.

THOMPSON: Are you a Reiki master? What is this?

MARK: Uhhhh.

THOMPSON: What'd you do next?

MARK: I put myself in her shoes?

THOMPSON: Come again?

CHRISTINE *takes a bite of popcorn chicken.*

MARK: I took a deep breath and put myself in her shoes. *I saw her.* Lower-class, clearly poor, over-dressed, heavily made up, perfume—her shoes . . . I had seen her shoes before, but I remembered them then. Her tiny feet. No hose. Barefoot in flats. I thought about her—

CHRISTINE *begins to cough, and to save herself she speaks.*

CHRISTINE: Julie and I are going to St. Barts this weekend.

THOMPSON: Huh.

(*looking to* JULIE) Just you two girls?

LAWRENCE: Every Mother's Day weekend, the two of them go travelling.

CHRISTINE: Yeah, we've been doing this for about seven years now. Both our moms passed away. Cancer. It was small, at first, and now it's gotten bigger.

JULIE: Missus Charter, uhhh . . . if'n you gonna need me to travel witchya, uhhhh . . . I'mma have to talk to Mistah Gordon. I ain't never been on no plane befo'! An' m' husban'.

Beat.

THOMPSON: Sorry, Mark. Crying. Breathing. You're putting her shoes on, you're putting your shoes on. I'm kidding. You're a poet!

MARK: Maybe?

THOMPSON: (*joking*) Mark Gordon, Criminal Defence Lawyer Poet. That wasn't in the article.

PRECY enters the living room and pours glasses of water for THOMPSON and CHRISTINE. THOMPSON drinks. PRECY exits into the kitchen and continues prepping food.

MARK: She was *only* nineteen years old . . .

JULIE: Food'll be served in one minute! Get yo' seats!

JULIE exits into the kitchen. She continues prepping food.

THOMPSON: Keep going!

MARK: And high. They were both very, very high.

THOMPSON: Yes, you mentioned that. He'll get seven years, do four. Tops.

MARK: I think so too. So. I say to the girl, "It's all right, it's cool."

THOMPSON: "It's cool."

MARK: Well . . . She is visibly upset.

THOMPSON: "It's cool"?

MARK: Yes?

THOMPSON: I don't think I've ever heard a lawyer say "it's cool."

MARK: Ha ha! Is that bad?

THOMPSON: It's interesting. Continue.

MARK: I'm looking at her and wondering, real tears? Fake tears?

THOMPSON: You size them up.

MARK: I guess. I'm in the moment. It doesn't matter because all of a sudden she's accusing me of patronizing her.

THOMPSON: Patronizing her.

MARK: I slowly take a few steps back . . .

THOMPSON: An accusation?

MARK: My hands still in their pockets—because—

THOMPSON: An actual accusation?

MARK: Yes.

THOMPSON: The judge let that happen? What a mess!

(*to* LAWRENCE) Too bad you've retired.

LAWRENCE: Sometimes I wish I hadn't!

    LAWRENCE *laughs.*

THOMPSON: You'd never let that happen in your courtroom.

(*to* MARK) She made a scene?

MARK: It turned into a scene! It was as if my silence gave her permission to show vulnerability. And she became afraid of her vulnerability and turned on me.

THOMPSON: She became afraid of her vulnerability? Very observant of you.

MARK: Thanks? So. She's accusing me of patronizing her. I take a few steps back. Put my hands in my pockets. Because that's the kind of guy I am.

THOMPSON: Safe?

MARK: I guess?

PRECY enters with her salad and warmed bread. JULIE enters with salad and biscuits. PRECY places it down and exits back to the kitchen. JULIE puts her food down and takes PRECY's food off the table and back into the kitchen.

She was scared. She probably loved her boyfriend, but you can't consent if you're high.

LAWRENCE: Yes, and they were both high.

MARK: She didn't want him to do time.

THOMPSON: Of course.

MARK: My client was in the room. And I gather . . . I . . . don't think anyone had ever listened to her before.

THOMPSON: No.

MARK: Really listened, you know what I mean?

THOMPSON: You're empathetic.

MARK: You think so? Thanks.

PRECY enters with the greens and the mashed potatoes. JULIE also enters with coleslaw. PRECY places them down and JULIE does the same.

THOMPSON: Something smells savoury. Is that—

LAWRENCE: Precy is a fabulous chef.

JULIE: No, suh. I's been cookin' all day.

LAWRENCE: Julie's been doing a lot of research . . . online . . . recipe books!

JULIE: No, suh. You *know*, suh! Uh . . . I don't need no recipe book.

(*to* THOMPSON) I's been cookin' for the Gordons for uh . . . fourteen years, suh! From scratch.

THOMPSON: You didn't have to go all out.

    PRECY *enters the kitchen.* MARK *goes to* CHRISTINE.

JULIE: (*to* THOMPSON) Gots a few more comin'! Be patient, suh!

THOMPSON: (*to* LAWRENCE) I don't know how much longer I can stay.

LAWRENCE: Mark, did you want to finish up your story?

    JULIE *walks briskly into the kitchen.* THOMPSON *sees the portrait of Gloria. He approaches it.*

THOMPSON: Gloria, right?

LAWRENCE: Yes.

THOMPSON: Beautiful.

LAWRENCE: Yes.

THOMPSON: Regal. Lost your queen . . . to cancer, was it?

JULIE and PRECY enter with their final bowls. JULIE sets her dish down and PRECY does the same.

LAWRENCE: She passed a few years after the kids were born.

THOMPSON pulls out a chair for CHRISTINE.

THOMPSON: *(to CHRISTINE)* After the wedding, you two will be having babies, I'm sure.

MARK laughs uncomfortably. He sits.

JULIE: I already gots babies, suh. I gots two babies. Well, they ain't babies no mo'.

LAWRENCE: Julie.

JULIE: They's big adults now. Able to come and go as they choose.

LAWRENCE: Julie.

JULIE: Can't tell kids nuthin' no mo'.

JULIE goes to the kitchen to get the Popeyes chicken.

CHRISTINE: Dinner smells delectable!

JULIE: Missus Charter, youse hungry, ain'tcha!

MARK: Come on, Dad!

JULIE: Yes. Suh. We got here some *good eats* this evenin'!

THOMPSON: Smells delicious.

JULIE: Mister Thompson, I's glad you could be here tonight to partake in my good eats.

THOMPSON: Thanks, . . . Cal . . .

JULIE: Calpurnia.

THOMPSON: Thanks, . . . Calpurnia!

JULIE sets the chicken down on the table.

JULIE: Yeeees, suh! We got coleslaw and biscuits! Over there is some fried chicken! And coming up for dessert is Massa Gordon's fav'rite key lime pie.

THOMPSON: (*smiling*) Your favourite?

LAWRENCE: (*lying, gritting teeth*) Yes. I love it.

LAWRENCE sits.

JULIE: Sho' does! He says to me, "Calpurnia, you mek sure you make some o' that ol' key lime pie fo' yo' Mister Gordon. An' Mister Thompson too!" An' I say, "Yes, suh!" Well now! Eat up!

THOMPSON reaches for a piece of chicken.

Y'all gonna pray, right?

Beat.

MARK: (*pointedly*) You love Jesus. Don't you?

CHRISTINE: Mark. Don't.

MARK stands.

MARK: Calpurnia, you must love Jesus.

LAWRENCE: Let's stop / right there.

MARK: Why don't *you* pray, *Calpurnia?*

JULIE takes her shoes off and connects with the ground.

JULIE: Yes, suh, Mr. Mark. Let's bow our heads.

Silence.

Dear Heavenly Father . . . Thank you for today.

Silence. MARK goes back to his seat.

Thank youuuuu. For the gift of food that we have here before us.

MARK bounds for JULIE. LAWRENCE stops him and holds his shoulders to prevent him from wringing JULIE's neck. LAWRENCE bows his head.

OH LORD! Thank youuuu! For the hands that prepared it! Thank youuuu, Jesus! For our guests! And may they be nourished! By this meal, as we are! Each and every day of our blessed—

(sings) Blessed lives!

(returns to speaking) Oh yes! May the Lord bless us! And keep! Us! All the days of our lives! Amen!!

All but PRECY—relatively at the same time:

ALL: Amen.   **THOMPSON:** AMEN!!!

THOMPSON waves his hands when he says "Amen" as if he is at church.

JULIE: Amen! Enjoy yo' meals!

THOMPSON reaches for a piece of fried chicken with his bare hands. JULIE dishes out food on THOMPSON's plate first and then she serves the others. PRECY goes to the kitchen to get the decanted red wine and white wine from the refrigerator.

THOMPSON: Nothing like soul food, hey?

He takes a bite of some fried chicken.

(lying) Flavourful.

LAWRENCE: I'm sorry, James.

THOMPSON: No, it's quite all right. Don't worry everyone.

(to MARK) Your case.

JULIE begins serving the biscuits and potatoes.

MARK: Okay, uhhhh . . . So. So. She is sniffing back her tears, the heat from the accusation has died down.

THOMPSON: Good, good.

MARK: I have my hands in my pockets. I'm trying to appear as safe as I possibly can, right? I *want* her to feel comfortable.

THOMPSON: Comfortable? Because you know she's lying? Comfortable because you want her to remember?

MARK: No, I just want her to be comfortable. I want her to know I'm safe to share with. My client had been high during the assault. I try to do that with every defendant. With everyone I come into contact with.

THOMPSON: What do you mean?

(joking) You're not a dangerous person.

MARK: Uh, no.

THOMPSON: *(joking)* I mean, do you *feel* you're a dangerous person?

MARK: No.

THOMPSON: *(joking)* Should we all run for cover or something?

    MARK *laughs.* PRECY *offers wine.*

LAWRENCE: Please try this. We have a few bottles in the basement.

THOMPSON: No thanks, reached my limit, thank you.

(to MARK) Basketball?

    MARK *and* CHRISTINE *decline.* PRECY *brings the wine back into the kitchen.*

MARK: No.

THOMPSON: Football?

MARK: No.

THOMPSON: No football?

MARK: No.

THOMPSON: Hm. I was thinking we could catch a game or something. What were you saying?

MARK: I just know that it can be scary up there if you're on trial and—

THOMPSON: New immigrant?

MARK: I don't know.

THOMPSON: I always keep that in the back of my mind.

MARK: Really?

THOMPSON: Yup.

JULIE: (*to* THOMPSON) How's everythin', suh?

MARK goes into the kitchen.

THOMPSON: Well . . . a little salty.

JULIE: Sorry about that, suh.

LAWRENCE: Stop.

JULIE: I am so sorry about that, suh!

LAWRENCE: All right.

JULIE: Here. Lemme take yo' plate.

MARK holds up a Popeyes bag.

MARK: Dad! *Popeyes?*

JULIE: *(anxiously)* Uhh . . . No, suh. Uhhh. I'll bring out the pie. You'll like the pie. I promise.

JULIE enters the kitchen. PRECY follows.

PRECY: You are making them sick!

JULIE enters with pie. PRECY enters the living room.

JULIE: All right, gentlemen. Key! Lime! Pie!

She flings the pie box.

LAWRENCE: Julie!

JULIE: Mister Thompson. You want a slice?

Jokingly, with an aristocratic accent:

THOMPSON: That depends on where you got it.

JULIE: Oh, you jokin' with me, Thompson! You good! You good!

THOMPSON stands.

THOMPSON: *(jokingly)* Calpurnia, you should cater our next garden party.

JULIE: Whut? A man like you. You don't got yo' own servant, suh? You don't got yo' own servant?

THOMPSON: My own . . . ?

(the accent falters) Well . . . yes. Yes. I . . . have a housekeeper. Yes.

JULIE: An' how would she feel if'n I came roun' the corner and was takin' alla her work?

THOMPSON: Well . . .

JULIE: She don' cook?

THOMPSON: She—ha—cooks.

JULIE: Suh. She wouldn' like that, and I wouldn' like that neither. Besides, I'm not sure if Lawrence here would want tuh share me!

PRECY: Hoy!

JULIE: Uh . . . Best negro cook this side of the county. Stealin' work from other servants. Uh . . . Ha! Maybe I'll come by an' teach her, maybe!

LAWRENCE: Julie Marie Gordon! Enough!

JULIE: Uhhhh . . . Well . . . well somebody . . . Uhhh . . . Imma get you a . . . Suh! Pie comin' soon!

JULIE goes into the kitchen to get a serving spoon.

LAWRENCE: You know how it is.

THOMPSON: Quite all right. Kids.

LAWRENCE: Doing things, trying things . . .

THOMPSON: Kids!

CHRISTINE goes to JULIE in the kitchen.

CHRISTINE: You gotta stop.

JULIE: You not likin' my meal, Miz Charter?

CHRISTINE touches JULIE's shoulder. JULIE flinches. She flees.

(prayerfully) Oh Lord. I did m'bes, missus.

(hurt) M'bes!

> *JULIE enters the living room with a serving spoon. CHRISTINE follows. PRECY stays in the kitchen.*

CHRISTINE: So . . . you can't come to girls weekend because you have a deadline? Or are you taking some time to research maid life in *To Kill a Mockingbird*?

JULIE: Miz Charter, I—

CHRISTINE: We *do* girls weekend to celebrate our moms, right? We go on a trip to celebrate our moms. Once a year. Every year. If something's changed for you . . . If you don't feel like celebrating your mom this way, then let me know. I'm flexible.

JULIE: Now, Miz Charter—

CHRISTINE: You know what? No.

JULIE: Miz Charter—

CHRISTINE: I am an ally! I support every creative thing you do! I may not be perfect but . . . you say you need a new copy of *To Kill a Mockingbird*. I buy you *six* copies of *To Kill a Mockingbird*!

> *MARK hands her the copy of* To Kill a Mockingbird *he was looking at. CHRISTINE opens it.*

(reads) Dear Julie. You're a writer. May all your dreams come true. Love, Christine.

She opens another.

Dear Julie. You got this. Love, Christine.

Opens another.

Dear Julie. You're an inspiration. Your words will change millions. Love, Christine.

And another.

Dear Julie. Keep going. I have faith in you. Love, Christine.

She unwraps the gift from earlier.

Dear Julie. Your mom would be so proud of you. Love, Christine.

Slight pause.

You're missing a copy.

JULIE: Miz Charter . . . I . . .

CHRISTINE: What?

JULIE: Miz Charter. I—I can't read those. You never learned me how to read.

(tearfully) You said youse was gonna learn me how to read!!

PRECY: I do everything!

(to JULIE) I walk you to school and carry you, no! Both of you at the same time! And your bags! In all weather! I cut your crusts and

make tiny little bread shapes with little eyes and whiskers and ears and feet and toes before everybody started doing it!

(to MARK) You cry for hours and hours and hours! I pick you up and you're a grown boy!

(to both of them) I rock you to sleep! In the night? I feed you!

(to JULIE) You don't like soggy blueberries, I take them off your blue baby-bear plastic plate and eat them like they don't bother me too!

As PRECY walks to her purse—

I have it, I have it. I like what you wrote Christine!

PRECY pulls out To Kill a Mockingbird *from her purse. She walks up to JULIE and raises it high.*

I? I am the one to teach you how to read!

She throws it firmly at JULIE's feet.

Me.

Silence. JULIE drops the facade.

THOMPSON: *(to LAWRENCE)* Thank you, I—

LAWRENCE: . . .

THOMPSON goes to leave. PRECY goes to the closet and pulls out his jacket. MARK is disappointed.

THOMPSON: Mark. Mark.

LAWRENCE: Thank you so much for coming over.

THOMPSON: No, no, it's all right. An art project. That's fine.

LAWRENCE: Thanks for coming down, James. Really, deeply appreciate it.

THOMPSON: Thanks for having me. Mark, we'll talk. Christine, it was lovely to meet you. Julie, you got me there. Tonya is going to—! We talk about this all the time!

Can Black people be racist? And there it is.

> LAWRENCE *clears his throat.*

That was by far the most racist thing I've ever seen in my life.

JULIE: Racist?

THOMPSON: The most racist—

CHRISTINE: (*quietly*) No.

JULIE: I can't oppress you.

THOMPSON: Well, you did.

CHRISTINE: No.

THOMPSON: She did.

CHRISTINE: No. Stop.

THOMPSON: Sorry?

CHRISTINE: No! Stop! Stop stop stop! I can't. She can't oppress you. Racism is prejudice plus systemic power.

THOMPSON: I'm sorry?

CHRISTINE: She doesn't have systemic power over you! Or me!

(looks at MARK) Neither does he!

MARK: Please don't.

CHRISTINE: When I say systemic power . . . You're . . . we . . . we . . .

THOMPSON: Say it! I'm white. They're Black.

CHRISTINE: Okay. You come in here and you're obviously looking for a Black man to fill your roster!

THOMPSON: . . .

CHRISTINE: Someone who reminds you of your friend?

THOMPSON: He reminds me of my friend.

CHRISTINE: It's a microaggression.

THOMPSON: Lawrence?

CHRISTINE: It's racist.

THOMPSON: Racist? I'm married to a Black woman. My kids are Black.

CHRISTINE: Right. Sure. And you can't be misogynistic because you're married to a woman, right?

MARK: *(to THOMPSON)* I'm really sorry about this.

CHRISTINE: No. This is not your responsibility. He's exotifying you.

(*to* THOMPSON) You're exotifying him! And just because you're a white man with a Black wife doesn't make that okay! It's weird!

(*to* MARK) I'm sorry, it's weird. I don't do stuff like that.

MARK: Christine. Please.

CHRISTINE: (*to* THOMPSON) You're upholding the system, upholding white supremacy!

THOMPSON: White supremacy. Sweetheart—

CHRISTINE: Not the Klan.

LAWRENCE: Christine.

THOMPSON: It's okay. I didn't think "the Klan." / I know we're not talking about the Klan!

CHRISTINE: Ughh . . . The legal, the political . . . the structures that uphold this country. What makes life so easy for me and you and not . . . not for the people you represent!

THOMPSON: We have a diversity officer at the firm. I don't need—

CHRISTINE: The things that break them down or kill their soul, take their joy, day after day. She can't buy pantyhose in her skin colour.

JULIE: I can.

CHRISTINE: Okay.	**JULIE:** Very expensive though.

CHRISTINE: Great!

THOMPSON *goes to leave.*

(*to* THOMPSON) No, no, stop, wait a minute. Do you teach your kids racism happens because . . . because of the colour of their skin?

THOMPSON: Yes.

(*looks around*) Am I wrong about that?

CHRISTINE: I'm gonna blow your mind. Just, just . . . Racism doesn't happen because of their skin colour—it happens because of what we . . . *feel* about their skin colour.

> She hones in on him.

Look, looook, it's me and you here. Just us—it's not their fault they're Black. We can't blame *us* on their skin. You get it? You don't get it. Okay, it's like this—

LAWRENCE: Christine!

> CHRISTINE *and* THOMPSON *stare each other down for a moment.*

CHRISTINE: Fine. I'll stay out of it. Fine.

(*to* MARK) I mean, don't you think it's weird?

> LAWRENCE *motions for her to stop. She pulls back.*

THOMPSON: Lawrence, we'll talk later, all right?

(*to* MARK) It's all right. Our diversity officer, Kiara Williams, book her, book this lady. She said that when we learn something new, we should sit with it, not try to change the world, until we're ready, until we get it.

(*to* MARK) She's got spirit. I like that in a woman. Marry that girl.

> THOMPSON *winks and then exits. Silence.*

LAWRENCE: Siri. Stop music.

The music stops.

MARK: Dad.

LAWRENCE: No. Julie, come over here. Sit.

CHRISTINE: Should I go?

LAWRENCE: (*to JULIE*) All of this is for you, and you just threw away everything I—

He calms himself.

All right. What did you *learn* by doing that?

MARK: This is *not* a teaching moment!

LAWRENCE: I will send you to your room. I *will* do that! I take my time with you kids. I put you first. I try to understand where you're coming from. A lot of room . . . for error . . . to explore . . . since you were born. So we will start again. What did you learn by doing that?

JULIE: I'm going to go change.

JULIE exits.

PRECY: What did *you* learn, Mr. Gordon?

LAWRENCE: Excuse me?

PRECY: What did you learn?

LAWRENCE: Perhaps we can talk about this later?

PRECY: No! No. No. Your parenting! Yours! I set the limit in this house. When you arrive, it is all gone.

LAWRENCE: I'm sorry, Precy, and we will talk about this later.

(*calling*) Julie?

JULIE: *I'M COMING!!!*

They wait for JULIE to return. She comes down the stairs.

LAWRENCE: Okay. Again. What did you learn by doing that?

JULIE: I learned that Calpurnia felt invisible.

MARK: Invisible? Really? Really?

LAWRENCE is mad at JULIE but is keeping it together.

LAWRENCE: Invisible? Can you expand on that?

CHRISTINE: Should I go?

JULIE: I felt small?

MARK: Dad!

CHRISTINE: I think I should go.

JULIE: Small . . . nervous . . . anxious . . .

CHRISTINE: I'm gonna go.

CHRISTINE stands still, stuck.

JULIE: Like, invisible. Calpurnia felt invisible!

PRECY: *You* think *I* am invisible?

JULIE: No-no-no-no-no. Not you. Calpurnia.

MARK: You're too much.

JULIE: I got pissed off. Mark, he—

MARK: Dad?

JULIE: Obviously I was figuring out what it was like to be Calpurnia!

MARK: (*to LAWRENCE*) You're not gonna—

JULIE: And! *And* you think my work is a joke!

CHRISTINE: I don't.

LAWRENCE: Invisible. Unseen.

MARK: You were the only thing I saw!

LAWRENCE: (*threateningly*) If you don't put yourself in your sister's shoes!

PRECY: (*angrily*) You know what, Mr. Gordon? You spoil these kids. They do whatever they want. You spoil them.

LAWRENCE: (*gently*) Thank you, Precy.

PRECY: (*forcefully*) You spoil them.

LAWRENCE: Thank you.

PRECY: Okay. This house. It's okay. My friends don't deal with this where they work. Just me.

PRECY exits into the kitchen. She doesn't clean a thing.

MARK: (*to JULIE*) The only person who's spoiled here is you.

JULIE: I'm spoiled?

MARK: Dad sets you up with everything, everything you want, all the time. And you blow it. Every time.

JULIE: I'm spoiled? Uh, Dad?

Beat.

Sorry to tell you this, but Dad sets things up for you behind your back. *Constantly.* All. The. Time. From time. All the time. He doesn't tell you because you're a guy. Sorry, a man.

(*to LAWRENCE*) If you think I'm going to keep covering for you, you're wrong. So.

They all look at LAWRENCE. Silence.

LAWRENCE: I asked Thompson to make you a part of his firm.

MARK: I know you love me.

JULIE: This is good. There's more.

LAWRENCE: I spoke with your boss, your peers.

MARK: My peers?

LAWRENCE: The judges. We talk.

MARK: *My peers?* I know you compare yourself to me. I get it. I get it.

JULIE: Yes. Yes!

LAWRENCE: The chances of you not being hired by Thompson are very small.

MARK: Didn't feel that way.

LAWRENCE: I know. He was giving you the gears a little . . . but . . . when I ask . . . *suggest* that things happen . . . For instance . . . I had the article written about you. Arranged the whole thing. Including the questions.

JULIE: And?

LAWRENCE: And . . . Your first firm. All me. And the second one. I basically . . . I basically . . . All me.

   Silence.

MARK: (*to* CHRISTINE) Did you know about the article?

CHRISTINE: I found out this morning. I'm sorry.

MARK: Precy?

PRECY: Leave me out of it.

CHRISTINE: So sorry.

LAWRENCE: I want you kids to be successful! I want you in a better firm.

MARK: I loved the people I worked with.

LAWRENCE: You can do better.

MARK: Both firms were excellent places to—

LAWRENCE: His firm will set you up for your entire life.

LAWRENCE sits at the table.

MARK: You're messing me up, man! You're playing with my gut. I knew it was you the whole time, of course I did! But . . . I wanted to think that there were still . . . parts of me that . . . they'd want? Being a lawyer isn't hard for me! I watched you! What if I wanted to be a public defender?

LAWRENCE: You have a right to be mad, but you'd never—

MARK: Been thinking about it.

Beat.

When Julie is being a jerk, stop her from being a jerk. Jerk move.

JULIE: That Thompson guy was a jerk.

MARK: You have to stand up to us, Dad. Or leave us alone. Leave me alone.

JULIE: You don't think that guy was a jerk?

MARK: No.

CHRISTINE: Seriously? He was so entitled!

MARK: It was an interview.

CHRISTINE: He was sizing you up!

MARK: You gotta stop doing everything for us.

CHRISTINE: That guy was the epitome of white privilege!

JULIE: Yup.

CHRISTINE: I'll reach out to him.

MARK & LAWRENCE: No!   **JULIE:** Okay!

> CHRISTINE *gives the family some space.* MARK *kneels at* LAWRENCE'*s feet.*

MARK: I love you. I know that Julie and I . . . It's all on you. But you know this isn't working.

(*to* JULIE) Is it working?

JULIE: . . .

MARK: You're retired. Rest. Chill.

LAWRENCE: You say that now but . . .

MARK: We're good. We don't need you to do all this behind-the-scenes business.

(*gently*) I don't need you in that way.

> LAWRENCE *stands.*

In that way, in *that* way.

JULIE: Dad?

> LAWRENCE *exits.* MARK *stands.*

MARK: Precy, you okay?

JULIE: Okay, oh kayyyy.

MARK: Precy.

PRECY: . . .

JULIE: Okay. I had a long discussion with Dad about the study of Black stereotypes.

MARK: (*to* PRECY) You okay?

PRECY: It's fine.

JULIE: He's the one who actually encouraged me to reflect on Calpurnia, to get in there, to understand her, do whatever it takes to—

MARK: Precy likes to peel every string off a tangerine before she eats it.

JULIE: All that was mammy culture. That's it!

MARK: Precy makes collages from magazines.

JULIE: Me performing mammy culture and the work that Precy does in our home are two totally different things. They are not the same.

MARK: She taught me how to scrapbook.

(*to* PRECY) On behalf of the family, I apologize for what Julie did. We're sorry. That wasn't very nice.

(*to* JULIE) You live in extremes. No grey zones.

> PRECY *folds a washcloth into a tiny square.*

JULIE: I'm trying to write about anti-Black racism.

MARK: The Gordons are better than this.

JULIE: No, we're not. We're just people.

MARK: You're better than this.

JULIE: You know what? Your respectability politics don't work with me! You're not Blacker than me because you visit Jamaica every six months!

MARK: Whatever!

JULIE: You're not!

MARK: No, I'm not!

JULIE: You're not!

MARK: (*in patois*) Me say m'not! Yu nah hear me say m'not, so if I say m'not, m'not!

JULIE: And I can write whatever I want!

   Beat. MARK *sees her.*

MARK: (*resigned*) Of course you can.

   MARK *looks for his phone. He searches his person and then other places.*

CHRISTINE: You don't think he was being racist about the trips to Jamaica—

MARK: Nope!

CHRISTINE: The food—

MARK: Nope!

CHRISTINE: The "dangerous" stuff?

MARK: That bugged me but—

CHRISTINE: I thought he was racializing you because he has a bias towards Black men. Like maybe he talks about this with his kids but that doesn't mean he can talk about it with you.

MARK looks between cushions.

MARK: Don't want to work with him anyway.

CHRISTINE: You don't think he's a white supremacist?

MARK: All these words, words, words! How are we supposed to survive all these terms, for fuck's sakes?! I'm trying to have a career, Christine! Leave it alone!

Where's my phone?

MARK exits. Silence.

CHRISTINE: Lee Lee?

JULIE: *(whispers)* I just need a moment to myself. One moment. Please?

MARK enters with CHRISTINE's coat and purse.

MARK: Found it.

CHRISTINE: Why won't you share things with me?

He gives CHRISTINE her purse and helps her with her jacket.

MARK: Let's talk about this at home.

CHRISTINE: Talk about race with me. I can handle it.

MARK: Can we talk at home? I'm gonna get some lumpia. You want some?

CHRISTINE: No thanks. *I'm your partner.* We can talk about anything.

MARK: Yes, we'll talk about it later.

JULIE: (*remorseful*) Sorry, Mark.

   Pause.

MARK: There she is. Remorse.

   MARK exits out the front door without taking any lumpia. Silence.

CHRISTINE: Can I ask you that question now?

JULIE: Sure.

CHRISTINE: It's the question from this morning.

JULIE: Okay.

CHRISTINE: So Black maids. Black families. Black life. Anti-Black racism.

JULIE: . . .

CHRISTINE: And Atticus Finch?

JULIE: Yep.

CHRISTINE: Why do you think you can write white characters?

JULIE: I've been studying white folks my whole life. Watching y'all on TV, film . . . Reading books about you in school.

CHRISTINE: Huh . . . Yeah . . . I always wanted to ask that.

JULIE: It's like I have a degree or something. Can I ask you a question?

CHRISTINE: (*worried*) Sure . . . uh . . . I . . . no no, okay.

JULIE: How do you feel about the phrase "the N word"?

CHRISTINE: It's better than the actual word?

JULIE: The slur is still there. No one is a racial slur. If someone thinks it, that means that they believe that people are racial slurs. If you believe someone is a racial slur then—I mean, my God, remember how mad you were when I *racial-slurred* you by calling you white?

CHRISTINE: Yes! It was literally one time, and I was *offended*! I googled "Why am I offended by being called white."

JULIE laughs.

Don't laugh. I learn a lot from the Internet. Oh my God I was so scared! I can't believe I did that! Aaaaaa! Allyship is hard. But I get it. During our bike ride, I was like, why am I bringing up these awful racist moments to prove your point? My intention doesn't matter because of my impact.

JULIE: Your reaction takes up all the space. I need to be able to get mad or feel sad.

CHRISTINE: I'm the worst. I read somewhere that white people are conditioned to think that Black women are angry all the time. So, like, even when they are a little bit angry, we're like, "Whoa, you're so angryyyy!"

JULIE: So this is you centring yourself, again, telling me things I already know about.

CHRISTINE: I'm so sorry.

JULIE: All I really wanted to say . . .

CHRISTINE: (whispers) I'm sorry. Centring myself. I just feel so bad.

JULIE: Huh.

CHRISTINE: What?

JULIE: I just . . . I'm not teaching you anymore. I need space.

CHRISTINE: I didn't mean to set you off.

JULIE: I've been speaking so softly. This whole time. I'm just telling you how I feel.

Silence.

CHRISTINE: (mimicking LAWRENCE) "If you don't put yourself in your sister's shoes. If you don't put yourself in your sister's shoes." Your dad!

JULIE: Yeah. He's, like, in love with Atticus Finch. Always putting himself—

CHRISTINE: Totally. But, like, if I put myself in your shoes . . . What I did was the worst . . . and soooo . . . I'm not going to do that anymore. Okay?

JULIE: . . .

CHRISTINE: I do my homework. Fast.

MARK: (*calling*) Christine!

CHRISTINE: But seriously, "You never learned me how to read"! Can't believe you did that!

MARK: (*calling*) Christine!

JULIE: I need space.

CHRISTINE: This is me giving you space.

> *CHRISTINE does a quirky exit. JULIE smiles. CHRISTINE re-enters to see the smile.*

Yeah I did. Impact!

> *CHRISTINE exits. Silence. PRECY gets her coat.*

PRECY: You copied me.

JULIE: I wish you could understand.

PRECY: You took over my meal.

JULIE: I'm so, so sorry. I got carried away. I was mad at Mark and—

PRECY: You made fun.

JULIE: Mammy culture is not you, Precy.

PRECY: For if ye forgive men their trespasses, your Heavenly Father will also forgive you. I will forgive you.

Silence.

JULIE: You know, I hear what you say underneath what you say. Black men always being arrested? Mark and Christine's babies, they're going to be so pretty? Stay out of the sun?

PRECY: Pardon me?

JULIE: It's just—I hear what you say underneath what you say.

PRECY: What do I say? You're mad at me now?

JULIE: No, actually, I'm not. I'm more sad at you, to be honest.

PRECY goes to the closet and gets her purse.

PRECY: None of my community go through things like this! None of my friends!

JULIE: None of your friends work for Black families, I bet. Is that true?

PRECY: . . .

JULIE: I thought you . . . Maybe a part of you . . .

PRECY: In the eyes of God, we are all one people!

JULIE: I know you love us but . . . maybe you . . .

PRECY: One people!

JULIE: . . . don't?

PRECY: Oh stop all this! One people!

JULIE: Yeah, but I'm here and this is now . . . I know this is a weird ask but . . . Do you love us?

PRECY: All these questions!

She looks at JULIE and then exits. JULIE watches her leave. She looks at her mother's portrait.

The End.

AFTERWORD

BY TOBIAS B.D. WIGGINS

Calpurnia, upon its premiere, built a steady, inescapable buzz. It sold out almost all of its opening shows and quickly became Nightwood Theatre's best-selling performance in its thirty-nine-year history, with actors receiving electrified standing ovations at each curtain drop. This hype and excitement were especially impressive considering the emotional tenor of its main themes and the political work Dwyer asks of her audience.

Dwyer explains that she began writing *Calpurnia* in 2012, and while "time passed as I wrote . . . Black men in Canada were being brutally murdered by the police . . . Trayvon Martin had been brutally killed. Sammy Yatim was also brutally killed." Informed by a climate of increased visibility and conversations about racist violence against people of colour, Dwyer took up the difficult task of representing the intricacies of social injustice that are still not adequately addressed in mainstream media.

And in actuality, these injustices are invisible by their very design. Everyday racism, or the way that our dominant ideology is founded in white culture, is a more subtle form of social discrimination. Because of this naturalization, it can be a lot harder to address. This is especially relevant to a Canadian audience, for whom a national ethos of "multiculturalism" can lend to complacency and an inability to identify more systemic, hidden forms of prejudice.

Through the resourceful use of humour and storytelling, *Calpurnia* does ask its audience to do some heavy lifting, not only to consider how racism informs the very foundation of everyday spaces like our homes and jobs, but also how racism is inseparable from other systems like classism or sexism—a concept Black feminist scholar Kimberlé Crenshaw famously termed "intersectionality" in the 1980s.

For example, although Julie is clearly attuned to issues of social inequity, her inability to write the character of Calpurnia is informed by her own class location.Her frustrations and entitlement lead her to inappropriately question Precy at length, trying to derive an "authentic" insight into a maid's lived experience. And Christine, who is often hyperbolically white and privileged, is also sometimes able to speak the most fluently about racism. Yet she simultaneously has her worth measured in marriage and child-rearing potential by sexist houseguest Thompson, the inflated lawyer, who also eventually calls Julie a racist.

To be playful, I would say that the layered plot is a bit like a social justice *Inception*—just when you think you hit the deepest level, heart pounding, you get dropped through another couple of insights about power. And although the play is about the everydayness of oppression, it is also a clear commentary on how domestic conventions are steeped in broader legacies of racism—primarily through the creative use of the classic novel and film *To Kill a Mockingbird*.

These complicated dynamics certainly leave the audience a bit unsteady and unsure about how to feel about each character. Perhaps this is one of the things that makes the piece so uniquely humbling and real, since none are perfect, and all are prone to struggle.

Each of the characters strive to somehow manage their social location (their race/class/gender, etc.) with honourable intentions—from Julie, who is unquestionably woke but still getting her sea legs, working hard to develop and refine her own political thought; to Mark, who often denies obvious racism to survive as a lawyer; to Precy, who, although disapproving, tolerates the family's drama and provides an inordinate amount of emotional labour—yet all are susceptible to political "failures." The question of what a political failure is, however, Dwyer quite artfully leaves unanswered.

Calpurnia is therefore as much of a conversation starter as it is entertaining, which is a feat when broaching complex social issues like intersectionality. And because of this commitment to the political, there is no doubt that your own social location will impact your experience of the play.

The set of the premiere production was cleverly designed so that the audience sat facing one another, with all of the action happening in between. This was a tangible invitation for the audience to engage in dialogue, to see other people's reactions, and to consider their own. Were they moved by the same issues as others? Do they feel anger, delight, or shame? Are they laughing, and should I be? Experiencing *Calpurnia* as an ally, one may be inspired to have new conversations with those across from you; and as someone marginalized, you may get the opportunity to share a moment with a stranger who has undoubtedly had that same experience.

Artfully told, with the softening qualities of comedy and the power of unspoken truths, Dwyer has crafted a theatre experience that is compelling, provocative, and not to be missed.

Tobias B. D. Wiggins (he/him) is an Assistant Professor of Women's and Gender Studies at Athabasca University.

AFTERWORD

BY HAZEL VENZON

One day, in 2007, I was stopped on the street in Vancouver and was asked what kind of Asian I was. After what felt like a cement block to my skull, through bits of brain dripping off my face, I managed to say I was born in Winnipeg and my parents were from the Philippines. Satisfied, the man answered, "Ah, you're Filipino. I just lost my nanny. Do you need a job?" That question redirected my artistic focus to try and figure out how we got here. I won't go into the horrifying details of that instance, but I can verify from my experience that Overseas Filipino Workers (OFW) have it bad.

Today, OFWs are considered modern-day slaves, working without the respect, care, and rights they deserve, and are often found in vulnerable situations leading to exploitation and abuse. What I find so exciting about *Calpurnia* is Audrey's choice to frame the play around the *To Kill a Mockingbird* character—the Finch family's African American cook, housekeeper, and mother figure—who, in this play, parallels Precy, a Filipina domestic worker who works for the Gordon family. Precy never experiences the harsh injustices that OFWs typically face. She's paid a healthy salary, she has a safe and roomy home on the Gordon's property—independent from the main house—and is treated with respect. In return, Precy is professional in her work and has grown to trust the Gordons, who reciprocate genuine care for Precy, even extending this care out to her family in the Philippines. Precy is an emancipated migrant, who has established herself in Canada and does not/has not endured the unfortunate treatment that most do—someone who got lucky.

During rewrites of *Calpurnia* for the Royal Manitoba Theatre Centre's 2022 production (co-produced with the National Arts Centre and Black Theatre Workshop) Audrey and I spent time including more contextual nuances about OFWs, fleshing out how Precy is an example of the important role OFWs play in the Philippine's economy. It was important for us to unpack the fact that out of the one million OFWs, today, (largely spread around Canada) a majority of them are women.[1] These women give up the chance to see their own children mature. From my point of view, Precy was conceived with the notion that she was Mark and Julie Gordon's main nurturer and mother figure in their early years. Alternatively, she was not able to nurture and mother her own. Precy's unique worker-versus-family arrangement with the Gordons—and by extension their personal-versus-professional relationships—are reflected in and among the ease with which Julie and Precy speak. I respect what Audrey's provoked us to think more deeply about, how the complexities of these roles become even more compounded when two individuals—both of colour—find themselves in a standoff. Who has the power? Does race play a role in a domestic workers' workplace? When is a domestic worker ever truly seen as an equal?

On March 7, 2022, Philippine Statistics Authority released a survey that estimated there are a total of 1.77 million OFWs abroad.[2] Roughly estimated, the money that OFW women send back to the Philippines makes up 10% of the country's GDP.[3] With this in mind, I think Precy was intentionally written with an undeniable sense of positivity,

---

1 "2020 Overseas Filipino Workers (Final Results)," Philippine Statistics Authority, 7 Mar. 2022, https://psa.gov.ph/statistics/survey/labor-and-employment/survey-overseas-filipinos. "By sex, more women were reported to be working overseas, accounting for 59.6 percent or 1.06 million in 2020. On the other hand, 40.4 percent or 0.72 million were male OFWs. The same trend was observed in 2019, where 55.4 percent of the total 2.18 million OFWs were women while 44.6 percent were men."

2 Ibid. This number was drawn from the OFWs or Filipino workers who worked abroad from April to September 2020.

3 "Bria House and Lot: OFWs and Their Impact on the Philippine Economy," Bria, Nov. 2021, https://www.bria.com.ph/articles/ofws-and-their-impact-on-the-philippine-economy/. "OFWs have long been known as the country's modern-day heroes. Since 1980, OFWs have helped a lot in keeping the economy afloat with

embedded with gratitude for the opportunity to be employed without any risks of unemployment. As well, Precy portrays a type of servitude that is driven by an economic pressure from her family as the main breadwinner. Precy carries the financial responsibility that all OFWs face in order for their families to not only survive, but to thrive and succeed back in the Philippines. In most cases, these women's occupation and labour supplement the lives of their kin and whoever lives within that household: their parents, siblings, and their siblings' kin, etc.

I feel as though Precy's position as a cook, housekeeper, and mother figure becomes blurred by the end when Julie is left grappling to understand how Precy fits within the Gordon household. I, too, am left grappling. Does Julie understand the implications of her performance and how that affected Precy?

Julie attempts to reconcile this through a deeper conversation about love, proving how blurry the domestic worker's role is when we're made to see people of colour in positions of power.

> **PRECY:** None of my community go through things like this! None of my friends!

> **JULIE:** None of your friends work for Black families, I bet. Is that true?

> **PRECY:** . . .

> **JULIE:** I thought you . . . Maybe a part of you . . .

> **PRECY:** In the eyes of God, we are all one people!

> **JULIE:** I know you love us but . . . maybe you . . .

> **PRECY:** One people!

---

their significant contribution through personal remittances which hit an all-time high of $33.5B in 2019 and accounted for 9.3 percent of our GDP."

JULIE: . . . don't?

PRECY: Oh stop all this! One people!

JULIE: Yeah, but I'm here and this is now . . . I know this is a weird ask but . . . Do you love us?

Most exceptionally, *Calpurnia* positions Precy between two polar races—Black people and white people. Entrenched in a complex history between Blacks and whites in Canada—and displayed on stage—Dwyer shows us the implications of day-to-day instances of racism within a multicultural home,[4] playing out various examples of systemic racism. The banter between Mark, Christine, Thompson, and Julie (117–121) is stealthily layered. I could read this section over and over and still miss nuances of what's being said.

Through a complex weave of racist microaggressions and racial tensions, we witness the invisibility of Precy's role as peacekeeper. Inevitably, we're left to face the sobering truth of today's collective moment. A time when self-righteous activism can seem like one's responsibility to their family or to uphold relationships or is to be a tool used to prove something to oneself. Julie role-playing as Calpurnia was an act of radical righteousness, but she did not account for its cost—a big gag leaving wafts of racism in the air that seemed to only

---

4 Kimberly Matheson, Andrena Pierre, Mindi D. Foster, Mathew Kent, and Hymie Anisman, "Untangling Racism: Stress Reactions in Response to Variations of Racism Against Black Canadians," *Humanities and Social Sciences Communications* 8 (2021). https://www.nature.com/articles/s41599-021-00711-2. "At the same time, to the north, in Canada, there were notable assertions that 'racism does not exist in Canada' (Lum, 2020), bolstered by the pervasive belief that Canadians embrace multiculturalism (Dunn and Nelson, 2011). Nonetheless, according to a recent national survey (Neuman, 2019), the majority of Canadians acknowledge that racism occurs at least occasionally, and that Blacks and Indigenous peoples (First Nations, Inuit, and Métis) are especially likely to experience racism. There remains, however, little acknowledgement of structural or systemic racism (i.e., 'racism without racists'), and even less recognition of the impact of minor day-to-day instances of subtle racism (e.g., microaggressions), or behaviours that have been described as 'racism with a smile' (Jones, 2020; Kunstman et al., 2016). At the same time, these subtle or ambiguous racist acts are especially likely to undermine the well-being of members of ethnoracial groups (Jones et al., 2016)."

move around in space. What we're left with is a heavy farce that releases tension and pulls into focus the intercultural racism between Black, white, and Filipinx people.

Hazel Venzon is a multifaceted theatre artist whose work often circles her back to her roots. She's worked with Prairie Theatre Exchange, Royal Manitoba Theatre Centre, Theatre Projects Manitoba, University of Winnipeg, Art Holm, Manitoba Association of Playwrights, Rainbow Stage, Young Lungs Dance Exchange, Mammalian Diving Reflex, Volcano, Cahoots Theatre, fu-GEN Theatre, Soulpepper, Chop Theatre, Theatre Replacement, Belfry Theatre, Green Thumb Theatre, Caravan Farm Theatre, Boca del Lupo, Ruby Slippers Theatre, Rumble Theatre, Urban Ink, Urban Crawl, and vAct. Hazel is the co-founder, executive director, and artistic producer of UNI Together Productions.

ACKNOWLEDGEMENTS

I would like to thank b current Performing Arts, Black Theatre Workshop, the Cayle Chernin Awards, the National Arts Centre, Nightwood Theatre, Obsidian Theatre, Studio 180 Theatre, Sulong Theatre, Emmy Lynn Bacani-Tipan, Dr. Beverly Bain, Leah-Simone Bowen, Dionne Brand, Lisa Codrington, Taryn Dufault, Mariver Gapusan, Mel Hague, Catherine Hernandez, Caro Ibrahim, Jillian Keiley, Nina Lee Aquino, Sarah Garton Stanley, Kelly Thornton, Hazel Venzon, and numerous workshop actors.

Calpurnia was made possible through the support of the Canada Council for the Arts, the Ontario Arts Council, and the Toronto Arts Council.

Audrey Dwyer is a multi-disciplinary artist with over twenty years of experience working as an actor, director, playwright, teacher, artistic director, facilitator, and mentor. In 2018, Audrey Dwyer was named one of the eighteen artists to watch by NOW *Magazine*. That year, her play *Calpurnia* became a box-office hit on the Toronto scene. *Calpurnia* was named one of the five hottest tickets in Canada across the country by *The Globe and Mail*. Her writing includes *The D Cut*, an award-winning six-episode series on Crave and Shaftesbury Film's KindaTV YouTube channel. She was one of the winners of the CBC Creative Relief Fund to create a television pilot called *The Gordons*. She has been commissioned by the Tarragon Theatre to write *Come Home—The Legend of Daddy Hall*. Her libretto *Backstage at Carnegie Hall* was recently produced in Montreal. She's been commissioned by Nightswimming Theatre to write *The Generations*, an epic drama about the legacy of a Black family over many thousands of years. She graduated from the National Theatre School of Canada.